GREAT CHEFS of San Francisco

Also Available
GREAT CHEFS OF NEW ORLEANS
GREAT CHEFS OF NEW ORLEANS II
GREAT CHEFS OF CHICAGO

Library of Congress Cataloging in Publication Data
Main entry under title:

Great chefs of San Francisco.

    Presents the chefs and their recipes for the menu
selections they prepared on the PBS-TV series of the
same title.
    1. Cookery, International. 2. Cooks—California—
San Francisco. I. Great chefs of San Francisco
(Television program)
TX725.A1G717 1983   641.5'09794'61   83-45980
ISBN: 0-929714-02-4

Printed In Hong Kong —Seventh Printing

California's fertile land and the waters of the Pacific Ocean yield an abundance of ingredients for San Francisco's chefs. Local wines, fish, and produce are but a few of the products available. This bounty is matched by a diversity of cooking styles and international cuisines that provide an enriching interchange of ideas and cooking methods.

As you watch the chefs at work and read through their recipes, you will sense their infatuation with food. Their love of cooking is evident in the subtlety of their movements, in their sensual pleasure while handling the food, and in their continuing efforts to perfect their art.

One note regarding the recipes: The number of servings and the preparation time are listed for each dish. Certain recipes also include the phrase *note elapsed time*. This indicates that advance preparation is needed. Always read the entire recipe before planning your dinner.

GREAT CHEFS OF SAN FRANCISCO represents thirteen master cooking classes featuring outstanding chefs from the San Francisco Bay Area. Each program includes the preparation and presentation of a complete menu, including the chef's wine preference. The series was designed both to instruct the home cook in a wide range of cooking techniques and to provide the rare opportunity to observe working chefs practicing their art in their own kitchens. GREAT CHEFS OF SAN FRANCISCO brings to television for the first time the genius and artistry of San Francisco's cuisine.

CONTENTS

CONTENTS

CHEF BRUCE LEFAVOUR
ROSE ET LEFAVOUR

"*I* thought of an Englishman in India," Bruce LeFavour says in tracing the origin of his recipe for Bombay Madness. "He's almost delirious from the heat and dreaming of England's coolness. The recipe's a blending of those Eastern and Western influences, of hot and cold."

Bombay Madness may seem entirely too whimsical to be the menu creation of a serious chef. Yet it is perfectly appropriate as a favorite recipe from LeFavour, who enjoys writing poetry, has no formal culinary training, and is noted for both the daring of his cooking ideas and the solid good taste and satisfying variety of his restaurant's wine list.

LeFavour learned most of his cooking methods from books. His mastery of technique, his seriousness, and his success are evidence that a classical background is not essential to the chef who loves cooking. Indeed, his entire cooking career is marked by a willingness to rely upon his own resources and to set his own standards.

2

With but one semester remaining to earn his degree from Dartmouth College, LeFavour took a leave of absence. He is still on leave, but it was the Army that provided his real education by assigning him to France, where he learned about fine food.

Upon his return to the United States, he went to Aspen, Colorado where, despite his lack of restaurant experience, he opened the Paragon in 1965. From Aspen, he moved to Robinson Bar Ranch, north of Sun Valley, Idaho. He rehabilitated the old buildings in 1975 to make a guest ranch and restaurant. LeFavour supplied the kitchen with duck, rabbit, lamb, and produce he had raised himself. He even made his own butter.

In 1981 Bruce moved to California's Napa Valley, where he met Carolyn Rose. Together they created Rose et LeFavour, a small, pastel-shaded restaurant elegantly appointed with huge, comfortable chairs, delicate crystal, and numerous paintings. The kitchen, stuffed with hanging pots, bunches of garlic, cookbooks, and a tiny desk, is at the back of the building. Through the back screen door, beside the stairs where dogs drowse in the afternoon sun, a tiny garden blossoms with herbs and vegetables.

Although noted for its wine, the Napa Valley is also a cornucopia for the restaurateur. "The valley doesn't just grow grapes," LeFavour explains. "There are many new truck farms, and here in St. Helena is a little lady who raises the snails we use at the restaurant."

Three days each week, he makes the 120-mile round trip to San Francisco to buy fish and cheese. He composes the day's menu as he drives, basing his selection on what is available in the markets. Instead of using written recipes, he relies upon his ability to combine often-surprising ingredients.

The fixed-price menu might feature squab breast salad, chicken filets with asparagus, pork filets with garlic and horseradish, and salmon with port sauce. LeFavour also encourages a vibrant spirit of creativity in his staff who, like Ann McKay, his pastry chef, respond with such delightful creations as her Strawberry Cake à la Dacquoise.

In addition to taste, LeFavour is intensely concerned with the visual appearance of every plate that leaves his kitchen. A perfectionist, he bends in concentration over each plate, considering the exact placement of garnish and the artful combination of colors.

His blue eyes are alert to detect any flaw, and he continually intones the need for attention to every aspect of the restaurant operation. "That's what the restaurant business is about, tiny details." ✗

ROSE ET LEFAVOUR
ST. HELENA, NAPA VALLEY

3

MENU

VEGETABLE SOUP
Vegetable gelatin garnished with fresh garden vegetables

SALMON WITH ASPARAGUS SAUCE
Thin salmon steaks in an asparagus cream sauce

BOMBAY MADNESS
Filet of beef steamed over lemon grass, ginger and peppercorns, served with curry butter and a fantasy of accompaniments

ANN KATHLEEN MCKAY'S
STRAWBERRY CAKE À LA DACQUOISE
Génoise layered with double cream and garnished with fresh strawberries

✗

VEGETABLE SOUP

SERVINGS: 4
PREPARATION TIME: 2 HOURS (NOTE ELAPSED TIME)

VEGETABLE JELLY (STOCK)
1 large onion, sliced thinly
1–2 washed leeks, sliced thinly
2–3 carrots, sliced thinly
1 parsnip, sliced thinly
1 medium rutabaga, sliced thinly
1 medium turnip, sliced thinly
½ bunch celery with leaves, sliced thinly
2 sprigs fresh thyme
1 stalk fresh basil
6 stalks parsley
1 small bay leaf
2 cloves garlic, crushed
peel of half a lemon
2 whole cloves
6 stars anise
8 black peppercorns

At least 8–10 hours before serving, place all ingredients in a stockpot and cover with cold water. Bring to a boil, skim, and simmer for 20 minutes. Strain the liquid, return to heat, and reduce it by one-fourth. Skim carefully during the reducing process. Remove from heat and measure the remaining liquid. For each 2 cups hot stock, add 1 tablespoon gelatin dissolved in 2 tablespoons cold water. Add salt and white pepper to taste. Pour into flat pan and chill for 2–3 hours.

GARNISH
radishes, thinly sliced
carrot rounds, blanched
green beans, blanched and split
peppers, red and/or yellow, thinly sliced
leeks, shredded and blanched
small cucumbers, sliced
peas, blanched
broccoli heads

Use any combination of 4 or 5 cold fresh seasonal vegetables, cut thinly and shredded.

Remove the jelly from the refrigerator half an hour before serving. Let stand at room temperature to warm slightly (if it is served too cold, the flavor will be lost). To serve, scatter small amounts of vegetable garnish in soup bowls. Break jelly into irregular pieces with a fork and place on top of garnish. For each person, use ½ cup. Top with fresh herbs, such as chives, basil, or tarragon. If available, add edible flowers such as borage, onion, or nasturtium petals. Serve within 5 minutes, since jelly begins to lose form if held longer.

SERVINGS: 4
PREPARATION TIME: 1 HOUR

SALMON WITH ASPARAGUS SAUCE

SAUCE
1½ pounds medium or small asparagus
2 ounces unsalted butter
2 cups heavy cream
salt and pepper to taste

Wash asparagus and snap off white ends. Set aside all tops and half that number ends. Plunge the tops into a large pot of salted, boiling water and cook until limp. (Note: Cook slightly longer than for eating. If undercooked, they will not process well; if overcooked, they will taste earthy.)
   Drain thoroughly and, while still hot, run through food processor with unsalted butter for 3–4 minutes until smooth, scraping down sides of processor frequently. Meanwhile, chop asparagus ends to remove field cut and simmer with cream. Cook slowly for 20 minutes, then strain, pressing through gently. Just before serving, combine asparagus, butter and cream. Heat slowly to just below boiling point. Correct seasoning.

(continued)

5

ASSEMBLY

4 or 8 salmon steaks, ¾ inch thick, boned
2 ounces butter

Salt and pepper salmon. Melt butter in heavy enamel or copper sauté pan. When butter begins to brown, add salmon and cook one side for 30 seconds.

Remove from heat, turn salmon, and let cook in hot pan off heat for 30 seconds. Salmon will be quite rare. Place on towel to drain. Just before cooking salmon, spoon sauce onto heated plates; then place drained salmon on top of sauce and serve immediately.

BOMBAY MADNESS

SERVINGS: 4
PREPARATION TIME: 2 HOURS

4 filet steaks, 1 inch thick
white pepper, cracked
1 stalk lemon grass, chopped (or 1 bunch lemon thyme or chopped peel of 2 lemons)
1-inch piece fresh ginger, thinly sliced
20 black peppercorns, crushed

Remove steaks from refrigerator at least 1 hour before cooking. (Steaks should be at room temperature.) Press a generous amount of white pepper into surfaces of steak. Cover. To prepare steamer, place lemon grass and water in steamer with ginger and peppercorns. Boil 1–2 minutes to release oils and flavors of aromatics. When ready to cook meat, salt steaks and steam over vigorously boiling liquid for 3 minutes *only*.

CURRY BUTTER

¼ pound unsalted butter
2 thin slices fresh ginger, chopped
1 large shallot, chopped
1 small clove garlic, chopped
1 small green hot chili, seeded and chopped
1 tablespoon Garam Masala (see any Indian cookbook)
1 tablespoon curry powder (if Garam Masala is not available, use 2 tablespoons curry powder)
1 tablespoon lemon juice
pinch ground turmeric
salt and pepper to taste

Blend all ingredients in food processor until smooth. Reserve.

Bombay Madness

ACCOMPANIMENTS/GARNISH
pickled onions
cucumbers in yogurt and crème fraîche
fresh mint chutney
papaya slices
banana slices
other garnish

For the pickled onions, use sweet onions if possible. Peel and trim top and bottom. Slice thinly, place in stainless bowl, salt heavily, and toss. Leave for 1 hour and drain thoroughly. Bring 1 cup vinegar to boil and pour over drained onions. Reserve. For the cucumbers in yogurt and crème fraîche, slice 2 small cucumbers thinly, salt, and allow to set one hour. Drain thoroughly, pressing gently to expell water. Mix ¼ cup plain yogurt and ¼ cup crème fraîche. Add dash chili powder and mix with cucumbers. Chill. For the mint chutney, see any Indian cookbook. Other garnish should balance Western color and freshness with the Indian flavors. Possibilities include blanched carrots, green beans, zucchini, and okra.

(continued)

7

ASSEMBLY

To serve, arrange accompaniments around outside of heated plate, place filet in center, top with dab of curry butter, and serve immediately.

SERVINGS: 12–16
PREPARATION TIME: 1½ HOURS (NOTE ELAPSED TIME)

GÉNOISE
 8 eggs
 ½ pound sugar
 ¼ pound sweet butter
 7 ounces cake flour

Melt butter over low heat and set aside. Mix eggs and sugar together and place in double boiler, stirring constantly by hand until sugar has dissolved and mixture is lukewarm. Beat about 5 minutes in mixer on high speed until tripled in volume and pale ivory in color. Sift flour twice, then gradually sift flour over mixture, folding in gently. Add cooled butter at the last and fold gently but quickly. Butter and flour the sides and bottoms of two 9-inch springform pans. Pour mixture into pans. Bake in 350-degree oven for about 20 minutes. Remove from pans and cool on racks.

BUTTERCREAM
 4 egg yolks
 1¾ cups sugar
 ½ cup water
 ½ pound sweet butter

Combine sugar and water in a small saucepan over medium heat, stirring to dissolve. Wash down sides of pan with a damp brush and cook syrup to 238 degrees without stirring. Begin to beat yolks in mixer. When syrup reaches correct temperature, turn mixer to high and add syrup slowly to eggs. Continue to beat until mixture has cooled. Add butter bit by bit to yolk-sugar mixture and beat until fluffy. (Butter should be at a creamy consistency. If necessary, beat butter to soften.)

8

CRÈME ANGLAISE
 3 egg yolks
 1/3 cup sugar
 1 inch piece vanilla bean, split
1½ cups milk

ASSEMBLY
 1 9-inch génoise
 2 cups buttercream
 ¼ cup Eau de Vie Framboise (raspberry
    brandy)
 ¼ cup Crème Anglaise
 1 cup crème fraîche
 ½ cup heavy cream
 1 pint strawberries
strawberry leaves and flowers
12 fraise des bois with stems (wild
    strawberries)

Heat milk with the vanilla bean to scalding. Allow to cool for 10 minutes. Beat yolks with sugar and gradually add hot milk, whisking constantly. Cook in double boiler, stirring constantly until it shows a "rose" pattern on the back of a wooden spoon. Cool over ice water.

Cut génoise into 3 layers. Sprinkle layers lightly with 2 tablespoons Framboise. Flavor 2 cups buttercream with 1 tablespoon Framboise. Whip crème fraîche and heavy cream together to form stiff peaks. Add ¼ cups sauce anglaise and 1 tablespoon Framboise and continue whipping until stiff peaks form again. If strawberries are small, slice in half lengthwise. If larger, slice crosswise into ½-inch slices. Spread one layer of génoise with one-third of the buttercream. Arrange sliced berries around the perimeter of the cake, with the cut side out. Continue to cover the bottom of the cake with half the berries and spread with half of the whipped cream–sauce anglaise mixture. Repeat for second layer of génoise. Place final layer on top and spread with a thin layer of buttercream. Smooth nicely. With small star tip in pastry pipe, make attractive border with remaining buttercream. Arrange the fraise des bois on the perimeter. Garnish with strawberry leaves and flowers. Refrigerate 2–4 hours before serving.

Ann McKay with Strawberry Cake à la Dacquoise

CHEF RENÉ VERDON
LE TRIANON

*T*he large kitchen at René Verdon's restaurant, with its imposing battery of pots and pans, its long row of well-used stoves, and its cavernous storage areas, attests to the impressive size of this acclaimed San Francisco establishment. Le Trianon's grand proportions are matched by the passionate involvement of a husband and wife who seek to create one of the area's finest restaurants.

Their division of responsibilities is reminiscent of that traditional French family enterprise, the *tabac*. In those ubiquitous neighborhood bars, the husband usually attends to the mechanics of the operation, dispensing drinks, food and advice from behind his shining zinc bar. Behind the cash register stands the quick-eyed woman, supervising everything and everyone.

Although the scale of operations is certainly much larger and the purpose markedly different, that same spirit of cooperative labor is evident in Le Trianon. Yvette, René's French wife, oversees the dining room. She has brought her artist's eye for color and design to the lush flower

10

arrangements and luxurious appointments. An imposing space filled with chandeliers, a full bar, deep banquettes, and spacious tables, it is a room made for serious dining in the old manner.

René's kingdom is the kitchen. With his bright, serious eyes, substantial body, and unruly hair escaping beneath his tall white hat, René seems to be the epitome of a French chef. The key to his culinary mastery is in his hands. Strong, delicate fingers caress the food as though ministering to a child. In the hands are love, respect, and sensitivity for the food.

René's father was a baker in the Vendée region of France. René decided early to become a chef. After completing a three-year cooking apprenticeship and two years' pastry training, he worked for several well-known restaurants in France, including the Hotel Normandy in Deauville. Later, he fulfilled a childhood dream when he signed on the luxury cruise ship Liberté.

He then worked in various New York City hotels until appointed by Jacqueline Kennedy to design and supervise the kitchens in the White House. From 1961 to 1966 he was the Presidential chef. In addition to his practical experience, he has written two cookbooks and has been the recipient of numerous awards, including the 1980 *Chef de l'Anée* in the United States.

At Le Trianon, René offers a wide selection of traditional dishes enhanced by his deft, imaginative variations. Of course, the ingredients are the finest. On a corner table, French truffles await preparation. Dark as night, pungent with a mysterious, earthy odor, they cost $200 a pound.

Although not a staunchly conservative chef who values only established precepts, René does believe there are no completely new culinary styles. He speaks instead of evolutionary change and of the need for personal judgement. "Nouvelle is just basic. The sauces are still there, just lighter. And it is still an emphasis upon freshness. Now the vegetables are just a little more *al dente,* that is all."

Like many celebrated chefs, he is highly sensitive to the visual aspects of food. "Looking is very important. Food is 40 percent eyes and 60 percent taste."

As if to confirm his freedom from conventional influences, René is iconoclastic about wine. His views are indicative of his entire approach to the business of eating and may account, in part, for his continuing eminence among his fellow chefs. "The rules for drinking wine are ridiculous. Drink red wine with fish if you want. The use of wine is a matter purely of personal taste." ✗

LE TRIANON
SAN FRANCISCO

MENU

MOUSSELINE OF SCALLOPS AND SALMON
Seafood mousse highlighted with a white wine and butter sauce

CHICKEN WITH PINK AND GREEN PEPPERCORNS
Boned chicken stuffed with veal, mushrooms, and peppercorns, then baked and presented with a sauce of cognac and cream

GÂTEAU NANCY
Chocolate and Grand Marnier cake topped with Crème Anglaise

MOUSSELINE OF
SCALLOPS AND
SALMON

SERVINGS: 16
PREPARATION TIME: 1½ HOURS

MOUSSELINE
   8 ounces fresh salmon
16 ounces fresh scallops
   3 whole eggs
½ quart heavy cream
½ tablespoon truffles, chopped
     (optional)
   1 ounce butter, melted
salt, pepper, and nutmeg to taste
16 individual molds (or small ramekins)

Grind scallops and salmon (separately) in meat grinder or food processor, then cool half an hour in refrigerator. Place scallops in bowl with 1 egg, 1 egg white (reserve yolk for salmon), salt, pepper, and nutmeg. Put scallop mixture in food processor and run 1 minute. Slowly add cream until blended (about 3 seconds). Do not overblend or mixture will be buttery. Add truffles to scallop mixture and set aside. Place salmon in bowl with the other egg, 1 egg yolk, salt and pepper. Run 1 minute in food processor. Butter molds, then spoon scallop mixture into them. Put salmon mixture into piping tube and pump into center of mold (or simply pour mixtures into mold). Place mold in shallow pan containing 1 inch of water; cover pan with aluminum foil pierced with small holes to allow steam to escape. Bake in 350-degree oven for 30 minutes.

SAUCE
1 teaspoon shallots, chopped very fine
2 tablespoons vinegar
½ cup Muscadet wine
¼ cup heavy cream
½ pound butter (to avoid oversalting
   use ¼ pound salted butter and ¼
   pound sweet butter)
white pepper to taste

GARNISH
1 bunch spinach, shredded
1 bunch watercress, shredded
1 teaspoon butter

Put shallots, vinegar, and wine into small saucepan and cook until half the liquid is gone. Add cream and bring to a boil, then whip. Add butter in small pieces and whisk over medium heat. Remove from heat and adjust seasoning.

Sauté spinach and watercress in butter for 1 minute. On hot serving plates, arrange some spinach and watercress in a small circle the same size as the molds. Unmold scallop-salmon mousse on vegetables, top with sauce. Note: May use a combination of sauces to form design on plate (American sauce, genoise sauce, and tomato sauce).

SERVINGS: 4
PREPARATION TIME: 2 HOURS

CHICKEN WITH PINK
AND GREEN
PEPPERCORNS

CHICKEN
2 chickens, ¼–½ pound each
1 cup cognac
dash of thyme
1 small bay leaf, crushed
salt to taste

To bone the chicken, producing two servings (or globi) per chicken, begin by cutting down along breast bone, scraping along bone to keep meat intact. Disjoint wing and continue boning along wishbone. Turn chicken over and cut along back bone, carving out the meat from the bone. Disjoint thigh and continue to remove entire half of chicken with skin intact. Cut off wing at first joint leaving only shoulder bone attached. Scrape meat off this remaining wing bone to remove bone, leaving meat and skin attached to half chicken. Remove thigh bone, leaving meat attached to chicken half. Cut around knob end of leg, releasing skin and tendons. Press leg meat and skin firmly toward thigh so that 1½–2 inches of

(continued)

Chicken with Pink and Green Peppercorns

leg bone is exposed. Cut knob off end of leg bone. Repeat with second half of chicken. Marinate for one hour in cognac, thyme, and bay leaf.

STUFFING
1 slice white bread, crusts removed
½ cup heavy cream
½ teaspoon green peppercorns
½ teaspoon pink peppercorns (do not use pink peppercorns from South America)
½ cup veal, chicken, or white meat of turkey, ground fine
5–6 shitake mushrooms, diced (may substitute morels)
dash of nutmeg
salt and pepper to taste

Soak bread in heavy cream and crush the peppercorns. In a bowl, mix ground meat and mushrooms with the bread and cream mixture, peppercorns, salt, pepper, and nutmeg. Place 2 heaping tablespoons of stuffing into pocket of chicken leg. Fold breast flap over stuffing, then fold thigh flap over other flap. Press globi fold-side down on table so leg bone sticks straight up forming a pear shape. Place leg with bone up in greased baking pan and brush with melted butter. Bake in 350-degree oven for 30–40 minutes or until chicken is cooked through.

(continued)

14

SAUCE
1 cup cognac (leftover marinade sauce
   from chicken)
½ teaspoon green peppercorns
½ teaspoon pink peppercorns
1 cup veal demi-glace
½ cup heavy cream

In small sauté pan, put ¼ cup cognac and peppercorns. Heat briefly, cover, then remove from heat. Meanwhile, remove chicken from oven and place chicken in a warm place. Pour fat from chicken baking pan and place pan on burner. Deglaze pan with ½ cup more cognac. Mix together demi-glace and cream and add to baking pan. Bring to boil. Continue boiling until thickened, then strain through chinois. Add the rest of the cognac to peppercorn/cognac sauce. Flame sauce, then combine with baking pan sauce and reduce slightly. Adjust seasoning.

ASSEMBLY
vegetables for garnish
(carrots, turnips, string beans,
   zucchini)

Place one globi on dinner plate and surround with sauce. Garnish with par-boiled mushrooms and other vegetables. Place frill on knob end of globi and serve.

SERVINGS: 24
PREPARATION TIME: 2½ HOURS

GÂTEAU NANCY

14 ounces semi-sweet chocolate,
   crumbled
7 ounces sweet butter
2 tablespoons Grand Marnier
1 teaspoon vanilla extract
1 tablespoon almond powder
10 egg yolks
10 egg whites
1½ cups sugar

In a bowl put chocolate, butter, Grand Marnier, vanilla extract, and almond powder. Melt ingredients over double boiler. Remove from heat as soon as melted and whip lightly. Whip egg yolks with ¾ cup sugar until a white ribbon is formed, about 5–7 minutes. Blend into chocolate mixture with spatula. Whip egg whites vigorously. Slowly add ¾ cup sugar, whipping until lightly firm. Fold into chocolate mixture blending lightly as for a souffle.

Use two molds 10 inches in diameter and 2 inches deep. Butter and flour molds using parchment on bottom. Put half mixture in each mold and bake at 275 degrees for 1 hour and 20 minutes. Unmold and cool on rack. To serve, sprinkle with powdered sugar and serve with Crème Anglaise (see page 9).

CHEF JEREMIAH TOWER
SANTA FE BAR AND GRILL

*T*he study of architecture led Jeremiah Tower to cooking, and that early discipline still underscores his culinary efforts. After graduation from Harvard, he came to California in search of work as a specialist in underwater architecture. He found himself one evening in the restaurant kitchen of Chez Panisse, helping to make soup.

Despite never having worked in a restaurant, Jeremiah was not awed at the prospect of cooking professionally. Born in the United States, he was reared in England and often vacationed in France, where he learned about food and wine. "I grew up in Europe, and I remember the food. I knew what it had to taste like."

From that inauspicious beginning, Jeremiah has built a culinary career based largely upon the expedient of combining fresh ingredients in a uncomplicated fashion. It was a concept widely practiced in Berkeley, California during the seventies. The very simplicity of the idea can disguise its importance.

For years, American cooking had been uninspired. In this country, cooks were not aware of cooking trends in other parts of the world, but as people like Jeremiah and other Bay Area chefs continued their experimentation, they created a movement that became the touchstone of American cuisine. From their early work, an American renaissance has begun. As a result, chefs throughout the country are now developing theories for superb, regional American cooking.

Jeremiah recalls that because of the spirit in Berkeley, the chefs would attempt almost any daring combination. Soon, customers became involved. They brought new foods into Chez Panisse for the kitchen to prepare. Salmon, trout, mussels, even veal kidneys are common on many menus only because of the pioneering efforts in Berkeley.

According to Jeremiah, the real breakthrough occurred when he decided to begin a series of regional dinners at Chez Panisse. The first, based upon California cuisine, was immensely popular. Praise from food writers James Beard and Richard Olney established the restaurant's reputation.

After working at Chez Panisse for five years, Jeremiah moved to Big Sur, California to cook at Ventana, then traveled to Europe to collaborate with Richard Olney on the *Time-Life* series of "Good Cook" cookbooks. He returned to San Francisco to teach at the Culinary Academy and to oversee the kitchen of a local restaurant.

Throughout those years, he was refining the concepts that would be important in establishing the kitchens at the Santa Fe Bar and Grill. Set on a busy Berkeley throughfare, the restaurant features white stucco walls and advertisements for the Super Chief, a prestigious train once run by the Santa Fe Railroad in America's Southwest. A full bar is prominent, as are a grand piano, large arched windows, and an appetizing display of desserts.

The kitchen bears witness to the restaurant's business volume. There are several prep and pastry rooms, large storage areas, and an enormous mesquite-fired grill and rotisserie. Since the emphasis of the Santa Fe is upon unadulterated tastes, the use of mesquite is vital to maintaining the distinctive flavors of grilled items such as chicken breast stuffed with tomato, basil, and pepper sauce; lamb chops with ancho and chili sauce; and salmon with red bell pepper–basil butter.

The selections are apparently simple, but Jeremiah contends that only the highest standards of quality and goodness will insure excellent foods. Innovation is the watchword for Jeremiah and, he says, for Americans intent upon developing their own cooking skills.

In an aside, he observes, "I think in this day and age what people don't realize is they can make a variety of things without a great deal of effort."

SANTA FE BAR AND GRILL
BERKELEY

17

MENU

SANTA FE BLACK BEAN CAKE
Mixed black beans and herbs, sautéed in oil, and served with sour cream and salsa

POACHED FISH WITH TOMATOES AND PURPLE BASIL
Filet of halibut poached in fish broth and served with tomato and purple basil sauce

SPIT-ROASTED SUCKLING PIG WITH SANTA FE BABY GARDEN VEGETABLES
Suckling pig flavored with oil, garlic, herbs, and lime juice, roasted over mesquite fire, and served with assorted baby vegetables

GRILLED GOAT CHEESE IN VINE LEAVES
Goat cheese and tomato wrapped in vine leaf and baked

WARM MIXED BERRY COMPOTE
Strawberries, raspberries, and blueberries mixed with sugar syrup and served with ice cream

RASPBERRY AND FIG GRATIN
Fresh fruit and sour cream sprinkled with brown sugar then lightly seared in broiler

✗

SERVINGS: 4
PREPARATION TIME: 30 MINUTES

SANTA FE BLACK
BEAN CAKE

1 pound black turtle beans, cleaned and rinsed
1 small onion, coarsely chopped
2 slices bacon or pancetta
1 quart stock, chicken or duck
2 Serrano chilies, seeded and finely chopped
2 tablespoons Ancho chili powder
1 tablespoon cumin
2 ounces olive oil
salt and pepper to taste

Using a heavy-bottom pot, heat 1 ounce olive oil, add the onions and bacon and cook for 3 minutes. Add the black beans and stock (just enough to cover the beans), salt, and cook until completely done. Drain well. Put beans, onion, and bacon through meat grinder or food mill to make a paste. Season paste with Serrano chilies, Ancho chili powder, cumin, salt, and pepper.

(continued)

18

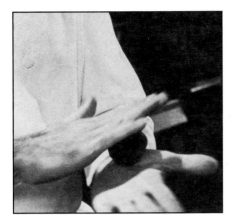

Take enough paste to roll into the size of a golf ball, then pound rolled ball between waxed paper until it forms a ⅛-inch thick cake. Heat a seasoned crêpe or teflon pan and add 1 ounce olive oil. On high heat, cook each side of the bean cake for about 1 minute (cake will be crisp and should slide easily in pan when done). Serve on a warm plate with sour cream in the center of the cake, salsa on top of the sour cream, and cilantro around the cake.

SERVINGS: 2
PREPARATION TIME: 20 MINUTES

2 halibut fillets, 6 ounces each
5 ounces butter, unsalted
1 cup tomatoes, seeded, skinned,
    chopped
1 cup fish stock
1 cup purple basil, chopped
salt and pepper to taste
parchment paper

Remove skin from filets. In sauté pan, melt 1 ounce of the butter, add fish and cover with fish stock. Adjust seasoning. Cover with buttered parchment paper, then bring to a boil and simmer for about 2 minutes. Turn fish and cook an additional 2 minutes. Remove from heat, remove paper, and let sit for about 1 minute. Remove fish from pan and drain on a napkin. Pass fish stock through a strainer to another sauté pan; bring to a boil over high heat and reduce by one-third. Add tomatoes and basil to pan, heat through, then add 4 ounces butter, salt and pepper, and whisk. Place fish on serving plate, spoon sauce over, and garnish with basil leaves.

Spit-Roasted Suckling Pig with Santa Fe Baby Garden Vegetables

SPIT-ROASTED
SUCKLING PIG WITH
SANTA FE BABY
GARDEN VEGETABLES

SERVINGS: 6–8
PREPARATION TIME: 1 HOUR   COOKING TIME: 6 HOURS

1 baby pig, 15 pounds
whole garlic cloves
1 cup lime juice
1 bunch marjoram, chopped
1 bunch thyme, chopped
salt and pepper
½ cup olive oil
mixed vegetables (bell peppers, baby
   eggplant, zucchini, summer squash,
   fresh green beans)

Rub pig with lime juice, salt, pepper, and chopped herbs. Put the spit through the pig, attaching the spinal column to the spit with some wire to prevent the pig from slipping. Skewer in place. (Put a whole bulb of garlic on each skewer before sticking into pig.) Roast the pig, browning the skin gradually. If the skin starts to blister, decrease the fire's heat. While the pig is cooking, baste it with olive oil flavored with marjoram and thyme. Cook for about 6 hours, then take the pig off the spit and let sit for 15 minutes. Carve and place on serving plate.

Bake the eggplant on grill until tender. Grill the peppers, then seed and slice when tender. In salted water, blanch the zucchini, squash, and green beans. Toss all the vege-

(continued)

tables in olive oil, chopped herbs, salt, and pepper. Add vegetables to serving plate and garnish with garlic clove halves from skewers.

SERVINGS: 4
PREPARATION TIME: 15 MINUTES

GRILLED SONOMA GOAT CHEESE IN VINE LEAVES

4 *fresh white goat cheeses, in rounds*
8 *pieces sun-dried tomatoes in olive oil*
1 *cup olive oil*
8 *grape leaves, stems removed*
16 *croutons, rubbed with oil and baked in the oven*

Gently pound tomatoes until flat. Dip rounds of goat cheese in olive oil, placing a flattened tomato on the top and bottom of each round. Wrap cheese with grape leaves (1–2 grape leaves should cover). Drip olive oil on leaves, then grill 5 minutes on each side. Serve cheeses on leaves, using croutons to scoop out melted cheese.

SERVINGS: 12
PREPARATION TIME: 25 MINUTES

WARM MIXED BERRY COMPOTE

1 *cup fresh strawberries*
1 *cup fresh raspberries*
1 *cup fresh blueberries*
½ *cup sugar*
½ *cup water*
2 *ounces butter*
vanilla ice cream

In a large saucepan, bring sugar and water to a boil, then simmer for 10 minutes. Add strawberries and blueberries to pan and cook 2 minutes. At the last minute, add mixed raspberries and butter to the saucepan with the other ingredients. Heat just until butter melts. Spoon onto a flat plate and serve with a scoop of ice cream in the center.

SERVINGS: 12
PREPARATION TIME: 15 MINUTES

RASPBERRY AND FIG GRATIN

1 *cup fresh raspberries*
1 *cup figs, peeled and halved*
3 *tablespoons brown sugar*
½ *cup sour cream thinned with 2 tablespoons milk*

Layer raspberries in a gratin dish. Pour sour cream over raspberries and top with figs. Sprinkle generously with brown sugar. Run under broiler to brown, then serve warm.

CHEF MASATAKA KOBAYASHI
MASA'S

*E*ach morning Masataka Kobayashi prepares at least five fresh stocks—two gallons each of veal, fish, lamb, game, and chicken. Each week he makes thirteen different sauces. That variety is necessary because every entrée leaving the kitchen of Masa's restaurant is flavored with two sauces. The range of flavors is absolutely essential to Masa's cooking philosophy. He uses sauce as a clothes designer might employ a brilliant scarf or a splash of color: to arrest the eye, to emphasize form, to heighten visual and aesthetic pleasure.

As a youngster in Tokyo, Masa was introduced to Western foods by his father, who encouraged his son to pursue a culinary career. At the age of twenty-one, Masa joined the Palace Hotel in Tokyo. His master chef has been an apprentice under Escoffier. Even today, the intensity and thoroughness of that early education are still with Masa. "My *grand chef* showed me so many things. I cannot change. Each time I make a dish, I think of him."

At the insistence of his teacher, Masa journeyed to Europe when he was twenty-six to train in Switzerland and then to work in various regions of France, including four years in Parisian restaurants. In 1973 he came to New York as chef at Le Plaisir, where he began to create dishes that were widely praised by restaurant critics. His influence was so strong that, when he left, Le Plaisir temporarily closed its doors.

Unhappily for New Yorkers, Masa did not care for the city, so he came to California in 1982 to work in a new restaurant in the Napa Valley. A year later, he was lured to San Francisco by Bill Kimpton, a developer who had long admired Masa's talent and who was building a small hotel near San Francisco's Union Square. With Kimpton as partner, Masa opened his own place in July of 1983. Its decor features brass trim, dazzlingly bright crockery, flattering lights, and several etched mirrors. Large bouquets add their sweet fragrance to a room already perfumed by the enticing odors of Masa's cooking.

With heavy eyeglasses, large chef's hat, and round, surprised eyes, Masa projects boyish exuberance. Using two chef's knives, he chops a rapid staccato over garlic cloves and herbs. Instead of adding ingredients in discreet, measured amounts, he grabs huge chunks of butter and tosses them into his sauces. Pushing his sleeves above his elbows, he works in abstracted concentration, fashioning his food.

Masa maintains that he is a visual chef, concerned with each tiny detail of preparation. That side of his personality is evident in the swirling cones of pasta reposing in brilliant red sauces, in playfully decorated crayfish, and in a skillfully arranged baby salmon, its pale meat accentuated by a lush, black line of caviar.

When asked to describe his cooking methods, Masa waves an indolent hand and asserts that for him there is only one cooking style, the classical. He is unabashedly governed by that tradition. He points out that in preparing his salmon he has used a red wine sauce, because "Escoffier said a red wine sauce with bone marrow for a fish dish is classic. Almost everything goes back to Escoffier."

With equal aplomb, he will also confess that his classical training is being altered as he becomes familiar with California's products. In San Francisco, he has no difficulty finding the fish and produce to spark his imagination. In developing his cuisine, Masa is conscious of reaching into his own years of experience, of recalling the instructions of his master chef, and of applying the classic dicta of the great French chefs. Then he adds his own contemporary touches, surprising with a flair and a sensitivity to the purposes, the possibilities, and the joys of food. ✗

MASA'S
VINTAGE COURT HOTEL, SAN FRANCISCO

CHEF
MASATAKA KOBAYASHI
MASA'S

MENU

GREEN PASTA WITH TOMATO SAUCE AND BASIL
Fresh pasta with tomato, basil, and garlic sauce

PASTA WITH CREAM TRUFFLE SAUCE AND FRESH MUSHROOMS
Fresh pasta with truffle, Madeira, and cream sauce

MEDALLIONS OF VEAL WITH SAUCE NANTUA AND WINE BUTTER SAUCE
Lightly sautéed veal garnished with crayfish and topped with two classic sauces

BABY SALMON STUFFED WITH CAVIAR
Fresh baby salmon stuffed with salmon and black caviar, and presented with a red wine sauce

WHITE CHOCOLATE MOUSSE IN AN ALMOND COOKIE SHELL
White chocolate mousse served in almond cookie shell with raspberry purée and crème frâiche

SERVINGS: 4
PREPARATION TIME: 1 hour

PASTA
1 cup flour (70% semolina; 30% all-
    purpose, rice or buckwheat) plus some
    for dusting dough during use of pasta
    machine
1 egg
1 teaspoon salt
1 teaspoon white pepper
2 tablespoons olive oil
2 tablespoons basil puree: 1 bunch basil
    washed and stemmed; purée with ½
    cup olive oil. Cover with a bit of olive
    oil and refrigerate up to two weeks if
    desired.

Place flour on work space or in the
bowl of a mixer. Add egg, salt and
pepper. Mix well, then add olive oil
and basil purée. Continue mixing.
Roll into ball and work by hand until smooth. Sprinkle ball with flour
and run dough through pasta machine. Dust noodles with flour and
do not dry before cooking.

SAUCE
 2 tablespoons butter
½ cup mirepoix (onions, carrots, celery,
    leeks)
 2 tablespoons shallot purée
 2 bay leaves
 1 teaspoon thyme
½ teaspoon oregano
 1 teaspoon whole peppercorns, crushed
 1 cup white wine
 2 tablespoons fresh chopped basil
 3 whole fresh tomatoes, ripe and
    chopped
 4 tablespoons tomato purée
 1 teaspoon garlic purée
 2 cups chicken stock
 2 cups veal stock
salt and pepper to taste

Melt butter in saucepan. Add mirepoix, shallot purée, bay leaves,
thyme, oregano, and peppercorns.
Reduce for 5 minutes (to allow
flavors to come out). Add white
wine and cook briefly. Add basil,
tomatoes, tomato purée, garlic
purée, chicken stock and veal stock.
Cook for 15 minutes (until vegetables are soft). strain into another
saucepan, adjust seasoning and reduce over high heat for 10 minutes.
Reserve.

ASSEMBLY

Cook pasta in plain boiling water,
then drain. In sauté pan, heat 2 tablespoons olive oil, 1 tablespoon
basil purée, salt and pepper. Add
pasta to sauté pan. Add a little
tomato sauce to pasta and heat. To
serve, ladle sauce onto serving
plate, swirl pasta in center and garnish with basil leaves and chopped
chives.

25

1 cup flour (70% semolina, 30% all-
purpose, rice, or buckwheat) plus
some for dusting dough during use of
pasta machine
1 egg
1 teaspoon salt
1 teaspoon white pepper
2 tablespoons water
2 tablespoons olive oil

SAUCE
 2 tablespoons butter
 2 tablespoons button mushrooms,
   chopped
 2 tablespoons shallot purée
 1 teaspoon peppercorns, crushed
 2 bay leaves
 1 cup white wine
 2 cups chicken stock
 1 cup heavy cream
 ½ cup Madeira wine
 4 tablespoons truffles, finely chopped
salt and pepper

ASSEMBLY

Place flour on work space. Add egg, olive oil, water, salt and pepper. Mix and roll into a ball, then continue working by hand until smooth and consistent. Dust lightly with flour. Run dough through pasta machine to form noodles. Dust with flour and reserve.

Melt butter in sauté pan. Add mushrooms, shallot purée, peppercorns, and bay leaves. Deglaze with white wine. Reduce over high heat about 2 minutes. Add chicken stock and continue cooking over medium heat 2–3 minutes. Add cream, bring to a boil, then reduce by one-third and make it a smooth consistency. Adjust seasoning. In another sauté pan, add Madeira wine to 3 tablespoons truffles. Reduce over high heat 2–3 minutes. Strain cream sauce into truffles and wine, then reduce to a smooth consistency.

Cook pasta in plain boiling water, then drain. In sauté pan, heat 2 tablespoons olive oil, 1 tablespoon chopped truffles, salt, and pepper. Add pasta to sauté pan. Add a little cream truffle sauce and heat. In another sauté pan, sauté 1 tablespoon sliced cèpes, 1 tablespoon sliced shitake and 1 tablespoon sliced chanterelle mushrooms in 1 tablespoon olive oil. Strain. To serve, ladle sauce onto serving plate, swirl pasta in center and garnish with sautéed mushrooms. Top with chopped truffles.

Medallions of Veal with Sauce Nantua and Wine Butter Sauce

SERVINGS: 2
PREPARATION TIME: 1½ HOURS

SAUCE NANTUA
 1 tablespoon olive oil
15 small crayfish (reserve 6 crayfish for
    garnish)
 1 garlic bulb, cut in half
 1 cup mirepoix (onion, carrots, celery,
    leeks)
 1 teaspoon peppercorns, crushed
 1 bay leaf
 4 tablespoons button mushrooms,
    chopped
½ cup cognac
 1 cup tomatoes, chopped
 2 tablespoons parsley, chopped
 1 tablespoon tarragon, chopped
½ cup tomato purée
 4 cups fish stock
½ cup cream
salt and pepper
cayenne pepper

Heat olive oil in sauté pan over medium heat. When oil is very hot,
add live crayfish and sauté for 1
minute. Add garlic bulb (halved),
mirepoix, peppercorns, bay leaf and
button mushrooms. Cook for another minute. Add cognac and
flame. Pour contents into a saucepan and mash with a spoon. Add
chopped tomato, parsley, tarragon
and tomato purée. Deglaze sauté
pan with 4 cups fish stock (enough
so that it will cover ingredients in
saucepan) and pour contents of deglazed pan into saucepan with
crayfish and vegetables. Roughly
mash contents of saucepan again.
Cook (boiling) for 20 minutes. Strain
contents of saucepan with crayfish
through a chinois into a sauté pan.

(continued)

27

WINE BUTTER SAUCE

1 tablespoon butter
4 tablespoons shallot purée
1 bay leaf
1 teaspoon whole white peppercorns
1 cup white wine
½ cup whipping cream
8 ounces butter
1 teaspoon lemon juice
1 teaspoon chives, chopped

STUFFING

2 tablespoons butter
1 tablespoon shallot purée
¾ cup white wine
2 tablespoons button mushrooms, chopped
2 tablespoons cèpes, chopped
2 tablespoons shitakes, chopped
2 tablespoons chanterelles, chopped
1 teaspoon garlic purée
½ cup veal stock
salt
coarse-ground pepper
1 tablespoon chopped chives
2 ounces foi gras

VEAL

4 veal medallions (each ¼ inch thick)
coarse-ground all-purpose flour
salt and pepper
1 tablespoon olive oil

GARNISH

1 tablespoon butter
1 tablespoon olive oil
15 leaves fresh spinach
4 small zucchini, peeled
4 asparagus tips

Reduce by two-thirds. Add cream, salt, pepper, and cayenne pepper. Reduce another 5–10 minutes to one-half. Strain and reserve.

In sauté pan, melt butter over medium heat. Add shallot purée and sauté for 1 minute. Add crushed bay leaf and whole white peppercorns. Deglaze with 1 cup white wine. Reduce by two-thirds over medium heat (*not* until dry). Add whipping cream. Add butter a quarter at a time, and whip briskly over high heat. Strain through chinois and reserve.

In sauté pan, melt butter over medium heat. Add shallot purée and let cook about a minute. Deglaze with white wine. Add all the chopped mushrooms, the garlic purée, and the veal stock. Reduce about 2 minutes (until liquid evaporates). Add salt, coarse-ground pepper, and chopped chives. Remove contents from pan to a bowl. Deglaze sauté pan with ¼ cup white wine and add contents of deglazed pan to stuffing in bowl. Add foi gras to rest of stuffing and set aside.

Salt and pepper the veal, then dredge in flour. Quickly sauté veal slices in oil (turning once). Pat extra oil off with cloth. Place spoonful of prepared stuffing between two pieces of veal.

Parboil spinach, and heat butter in sauté pan. Add spinach to sauté pan and cook very briefly. Reserve. In another sauté pan, heat oil. Sauté zucchini about 1–2 minutes. Reserve. Blanch asparagus tips and reserve.

(continued)

ASSEMBLY

Put stuffed veal on a bed of sautéed spinach. Garnish each plate with 1 crayfish head and 3 crayfish tails (boiled). Spoon sauce nantua onto the bottom of the plate. Add lemon juice and chives to the wine butter sauce and spoon over veal. Garnish with two asparagus tips per plate and 2 small zucchini.

SERVINGS: 2
PREPARATION TIME: 2 HOURS

RED WINE SAUCE
½ cup olive oil
1 pound salmon bones
1 pound butter
2 cups mirepoix (onion, celery, carrots, leeks)
4 bay leaves
½ teaspoon oregano
½ teaspoon thyme
½ teaspoon white peppercorns
4 tablespoons shallot purée
¼ cup cognac
2 cups red wine
1 cup fish stock

In sauté pan, heat olive oil. Sauté salmon bones for about 1 minute. Add butter (about 2 tablespoons), 1 cup mirepoix, 2 bay leaves, ¼ teaspoon oregano, ¼ teaspoon thyme, ¼ teaspoon peppercorns and 2 tablespoons shallot purée. Add cognac and flame. Deglaze with 1 cup red wine and cook over high heat for 5–10 minutes. Meanwhile, in a second sauté pan, melt 2 tablespoons butter. Add 2 tablespoons shallot purée, 1 cup mirepoix, 2 bay leaves, ¼ teaspoon peppercorns, ¼ teaspoon oregano, ¼ teaspoon thyme, and 3 cups red wine. Reduce over medium heat to dry. Add 1 cup fish stock to sauté pan with salmon bones. Cook about 5 minutes. Deglaze reduction (shallot-red wine) in second sauté pan with about 3 cups of strained liquid from the first sauté pan (salmon bones and fish stock). Reduce ingredients in second saucepan by two-thirds (not dry). Add remainder of butter, whisk, and add salt and pepper to taste. Strain and reserve.

(continued)

29

SALMON MOUSSE

1 cup salmon fillets (about 8 ounces per
  stuffed fish)
1 egg white
½–¾ cup heavy cream
1 teaspoon Pernod
1 teaspoon cognac
1 tablespoon caviar

SALMON

1 fresh baby salmon filet (about 5–6
  ounces), head, tail, and skin on
3 tablespoons caviar
1 tablespoon chives, chopped
1 cup white wine
2 tablespoons shallot purée
1 bay leaf

GARNISH

sautéed cucumber (cut into strings)
chopped tomato
chopped chives
salmon eggs
crayfish tails

Purée salmon filet in food processor. Put salmon into stainless bowl over ice. Add egg white and whip with spatula. While whipping, add heavy cream to a smooth consistency. Adjust salt and pepper, then add 1 teaspoon Pernod, 1 teaspoon cognac and 1 tablespoon caviar. Mix well and put in piping tube. Reserve.

Wash and salt and pepper baby salmon. Pipe salmon mousse into inside of salmon. Add a line of caviar to the inside of salmon, then sprinkle with chives. Close fish. In sauté pan, heat white wine. Add shallot purée and bay leaf. Place fish in the sauté pan (belly down) and bake in a 350–400 degree oven for 20 minutes. When fish is cooked, remove from pan, remove the skin and reserve in a warm place. Heat juices in sauté pan for a couple of minutes. Strain juices into a saucepan containing a wine butter sauce (see page 28).

Place baby salmon on serving dish. Ladle salmon-flavored red wine sauce over half the fish and the wine butter sauce (flavored with poaching liquid) over the other half. Garnish with cucumber, tomato, chives, salmon eggs, and crayfish tails (boiled).

30

SERVINGS: 6
PREPARATION TIME: 1 HOUR (NOTE ELAPSED TIME)

ALMOND COOKIE SHELL
 3 egg whites
 2 tablespoons sugar
 2 tablespoons flour
 ½ cup almonds, sliced and toasted

Put egg whites in bowl and beat briefly. Add sugar and flour, then whisk. Stir almonds into mixture. Butter sheet pan and spoon tablespoons of mixture onto pan. Spread slightly with the back of a spoon to form circles about 2 inches apart. Bake in a 350-degree oven for 5–7 minutes. Remove from oven and while still hot mold into small cups by placing over a rolling pin. Set aside to dry.

MOUSSE
 1 cup sugar
 ½ cup water
 8 egg whites
 6 egg yolks
 1 tablespoon white rum
 1 pound white chocolate, melted
crème frâiche
raspberry purée

In saucepan, heat sugar and water until it forms a soft ball. In the bowl of a mixer, put egg whites and beat until medium stiff, beating first on medium then on high. Add sugar and water (soft ball stage) to egg whites and continue to beat briefly until a stiff meringue is formed. Place egg yolks in a metal bowl and beat over heat with a whisk. Add rum to egg yolks—still beating over heat. Fold egg yolks into egg whites. Fold melted chocolate into egg mixture. Refrigerate 3–4 hours. Serve one scoop mousse in an almond cookie shell. Garnish with raspberry purée and crème frâiche.

31

CHEF MAX SCHACHER
LE COQUELICOT

Max Schacher named his restaurant *Le Coquelicot* because he thought the word gentle and melodious. In English, *coquelicot* is "poppy." These delicate yellow flowers flourish on the long ridges of Mt. Tamalpais, a graceful mountain overlooking the green plaza of Ross where Max has built a restaurant as light and airy, as colorful and peaceful, as the mountain itself.

Le Coquelicot is constructed within the walls of a rehabilitated automotive garage. At one end of the building is the kitchen,

compact, well-organized, and very clean. At the opposite end are glass doors leading to a small terrace set in the shadow of an enormous palm tree. The main dining room is both relaxing and functional. With its white tablecloths, simple sideboard, modern paintings, and lovely flowers, it is a fitting stage for Max's culinary art.

Born of Swiss-German parents in Lausanne, Switzerland, Max has been working with food since he was fifteen. An interest in cooking came naturally to the child whose grandfather and sister owned restaurants. Although only in his mid-thirties, Max has a surprisingly diverse background.

After his apprenticeship in several Swiss hotels and restaurants, he worked in Germany as a waiter, in France as a bartender, in England as a sous-chef, and as chef de cuisine in Tahiti, where he had sailed in his own ketch from San Francisco. At the conclusion of his three-year sojourn in the South Pacific, he returned to California to become co-owner of Chez Michel before opening his own place in 1982.

A sturdy, solid man who jokes easily in four languages, Max enjoys his work and obviously enjoys being with the restaurant staff. Affable and charming, he is an accomplished chef who also appreciates the subtle demands of the dining room. He knows that the kitchen workers must be mechanically perfect and, equally important, the dining room personnel must be efficient and personable.

He can discourse about food costs (his are extremely high because of the rarity and excellence of his basic ingredients) or about the proper lighting for the tables. Max's wife Susan attends to the public areas, where she supervises table service and acts as hostess, freeing Max to concentrate upon the cooking.

The Schachers are particularly proud of their menu. Composed principally of recipes devised by Max, it is a result of his years of work in European kitchens and his belief that his customers are willing to sample anything at least once. Traditional fare such as steak tartare with fried potatoes and rack of lamb are balanced with specials such as Max's Oysters Tahaa and Cervelle with Capers.

"When I first introduced rabbit a year ago, we had a hard time selling it. Now I go through many each week. Most Americans are always looking for more interesting cooking. Their minds are always open to different kinds of food."

Max believes that fashion too often dictates culinary trends. Education is necessary to avoid the pitfalls of experimental cooking. "A chef needs a good classic base to be strong; then he can be innovative."

For instance, Max is aware that herbs are currently in vogue, and naturally he has an extensive herb garden at home. But he has reached an intriguing conclusion about the use of herbs. "Many times you don't need to cook with the herbs because they are so strong they will perfume the sauce perfectly if sprinkled on at the end."

Max's use of herbs reflects his quest for intelligent refinement and his desire to create food that is a distinct, memorable pleasure to see and to eat. ✗

LE COQUELICOT
ROSS, MARIN COUNTY

MENU

MOUSSE OF DUCK LIVER

Flavorful duck liver mousse with cognac and shallots molded in a port-flavored aspic

OYSTERS SOUVENIR DE TAHAA

Oysters lightly breaded with herbs and served in a shallot and white wine sauce

SADDLE OF RABBIT WITH LEEKS AND ROSEMARY

Choice saddle of rabbit marinated in mirepoix, thinly sliced, then served in a sauce of rabbit stock, tomatoes and vegetables

WALNUT PIE À LA MODE

Le Coquelicot's vanilla ice cream over a freshly baked walnut pie

✗

Sous-chef Steve Papas, Chef Max, and pastry chef Cynthia Henderson

Mousse of Duck Liver

SERVINGS: 20
PREPARATION TIME: 30 MINUTES (NOTE ELAPSED TIME)
1 HOUR TO SET

ASPIC
2 *envelopes (½ ounce) unflavored gelatin*
2 *cups Madrilène (may be purchased canned)*
2 *tablespoons cognac*
2 *tablespoons port*

To make aspic, soften 1 envelope of gelatin in 1 cup Madrilène, then heat briefly with 1 tablespoon each of cognac and port. Do this twice–once for the bottom of the pâté mold and once for the top.

(continued)

MOUSSE

4 ounces butter
sprig of fresh thyme (½ teaspoon dried)
2 tablespoons shallots, chopped
2 pounds duck liver, chopped
1 cup port
2 cups heavy cream
2 envelopes (½ ounce) unflavored gelatin
½ cup cognac
dash fresh lemon juice
salt, pepper, cayenne pepper

Note: You may need to process the liver mixture with the cream in 2 batches if it's too full for the processing bowl. Consult manufacturer's instructions for guidelines.

Cover bottom of standard loaf pan (9¼ × 5¼ × 3-inch) with 1 cup aspic. Put mold in refrigerator and let sit until hard, approximately 15 minutes. In large sauté pan, slowly cook butter, thyme, and shallots for 2 minutes. Add duck liver and cook until rare. Salt and pepper to taste. Add port, flame, and cook for another 2 minutes. Pour mixture into bowl of food processor. In a sauté pan, heat all but ½ cup heavy cream. Soften the gelatin in the reserved cream, then add to the heated cream. Add cream to liver mixture in food processor and purée for one minute (see note below). Strain through fine sieve into large bowl. Whisk. Add cognac, lemon juice, salt, pepper, and cayenne to taste. Mix thoroughly, place in mold and cool for 2 hours in the refrigerator. Pour remaining cup of aspic over the top of liver mixture in mold. Return to refrigerator for 15 minutes until aspic hardens. Unmold, slice, serve on cold plates with French bread toasts.

OYSTERS SOUVENIR DE TAHAA

SERVINGS: 4
PREPARATION TIME: 30 MINUTES

OYSTERS AND BREADING

20 medium oysters
1 cup bread crumbs
1 tablespoon fresh mint, chopped
1 tablespoon fresh thyme, chopped
1 tablespoon fresh marjoram, chopped
1 tablespoon fresh oregano, chopped
1 tablespoon fresh shallots, chopped
1 tablespoon fresh parsley, chopped
2 tablespoons flour
3 eggs
1 tablespoon butter
1 tablespoon olive oil

Beat eggs in bowl and set aside. Add fresh herbs to bread crumbs and set aside. Shuck oysters and save juice and shells. Place oysters on dry towel. Sprinkle well with flour. Dip oysters into egg mixture and then into crumb/herb mixture. Place oysters on dry towel and put in refrigerator.

36

CREAM OF SHALLOTS SAUCE
8 ounces dry white wine
2 ounces lemon juice
4 ounces heavy cream
4 ounces butter
4 tablespoons shallots, chopped
salt and pepper to taste
reserved oyster juice

ASSEMBLY
4 half oyster shells
4 sprigs parsley
2 limes, cut in half
1 tablespoon chopped chives

In saucepan cook shallots, white wine, oyster juice and lemon juice until all liquid has evaporated. Add cream and bring to strong boil, whisking constantly. Whip in small pieces of butter until melted. Remove from heat. Season to taste with salt and pepper. Strain through fine sieve into another pan and keep warm.

In large sauté pan add 1 tablespoon olive oil and 1 tablespoon butter. Heat until butter sizzles. Add oysters and cook for 1 minute on each side until light brown and crispy on outside. Remove and place on paper towels. Warm serving plates. Pour sauce on plates and place oyster shell in center with garnish of parsley and half a lime. Arrange oysters in circular pattern around the garnish. Serve immediately.

SERVINGS: 2
PREPARATION TIME: 45 MINUTES (NOTE ELAPSED TIME)

SADDLE OF RABBIT WITH LEEKS AND ROSEMARY

MARINADE, RABBIT, AND SAUCE
1–3 pound rabbit (use only saddle
   section: the back from first rib to
   beginning of legs)
1 small carrot
½ medium onion
1 stalk celery
1 clove garlic, crushed
2 sprigs fresh rosemary
1 tablespoon olive oil
2 tablespoons butter
1⅓ cups white wine
1 cup rabbit stock or chicken bouillon
1 tomato, sliced
salt and pepper to taste

Put saddle of rabbit in a small bowl with 1 cup white wine and 1 sprig rosemary. Cut the carrot, onion, celery, and garlic into small pieces and add to marinade. Cover bowl with plastic wrap and store in refrigerator 24–48 hours.

Remove rabbit from marinade and dry with cloth. Salt and pepper the rabbit and preheat oven to 450 degrees. In medium roasting pan, add 1 tablespoon butter and 1 tablespoon olive oil. Heat until butter sizzles. Place rabbit in pan, skin side up, and brown. Turn, wrapping flaps around filet to protect it, and cook until light brown. Place pan in 450-degree oven and cook for 10 minutes, until medium rare. Baste often.

(continued)

37

Add vegetables from marinade to pan with rabbit and cook for another 5 minutes, basting and turning occasionally Remove rabbit from pan and place in warm location. Trim saddle flaps from rabbit and chop flaps coarsely. Return to pan with vegetables. On stove stop, sauté briefly and skim fat. Deglaze pan with ½ cup wine, add rabbit stock and reduce by one-half. Add tomato and sauté while stirring. Strain through sieve, reserving liquid (for sauce) and discarding vegetables. Add butter to liquid and whisk until smooth.

LEEKS
2 medium leeks
1 tablespoon butter
salt to taste

Julienne leeks. Rinse in cold water and drain well. In medium sauté pan add 1 tablespoon butter and leeks. Cook slowly for 2–5 minutes. Leeks should remain crisp. Adjust seasoning. Reserve leeks in warm place.

ASSEMBLY

Remove filet of rabbit from saddle. Cut saddle bone crosswise and place one section on each of two plates. Surround saddle bones with leeks. Cut filet of rabbit into very thin slices lengthwise. Fan slices on top of leeks. Cover with sauce, garnish with sprigs of rosemary. Serve immediately.

VANILLA ICE CREAM
½ quart milk
6 egg yolks
1 cup sugar
½ quart heavy cream
1 vanilla bean

WALNUT PIE
3 cups flour
1 cup sugar
1 cup butter, cooled
pinch salt
1 egg
1 egg yolk
1 pound chopped walnuts
3 cups heavy cream
2 cups sugar

Cut vanilla bean lengthwise into 4 sections and place in saucepan with milk. Bring milk to boil and remove from heat. In stainless bowl, whip egg yolks and sugar until foamy. Strain milk into egg mixture. Place bowl on double-boiler and mix with wooden spatula until mixture thickens and adheres to spatula. Remove from boiler. Add heavy cream and place in refrigerator until cold. Pour mixture into ice cream freezer and churn for 30 minutes or until stiff.

In large bowl, combine sugar, cooled butter, and salt. Add flour 1 cup at a time and mix. Add 1 egg and mix well but do not overwork. Divide dough mixture into ⅔ and ⅓ portions. Let rest in refrigerator at least 2 hours, overnight if possible. Roll out ⅔ portion of dough until 13 inches in diameter. Place in buttered 10-inch pie plate. Leave excess dough hanging over edge of plate. Place in refrigerator. Roll out ⅓ portion of dough until 11 inches in diameter. Refrigerate.

In saucepan over medium heat, boil heavy cream and sugar until reduced by one-half. Add walnuts and cook for 5 minutes. Pour mixture into bowl and refrigerate.

Remove pie plate from refrigerator and fill with cooled walnut mixture. Take 1 beaten egg yolk and brush pie dough around lip of plate. Cover with top dough, press around edge, and remove excess dough. Brush top of pie with egg yolk. Score dough with fork in crisscross pattern, then bake in 375-degree oven for 30 minutes. Refrigerate until cold and serve topped with ice cream.

CHEF JACKY ROBERT
ERNIE'S

*J*acky Robert's philosophy of cooking is that of a man who has worked his entire professional life in kitchens. He states that cooking is an art requiring a thorough grounding in basics and careful refinement. For him, the nuances define chefs. "A pinch of salt makes the difference between cooks. You must know when to add something and when to stop."

Traditional and contemporary cuisine are seen by Jacky as parts of a whole. His success at integrating his own ideas with classic culinary precepts is evident in the intriguing menu at Ernie's Restaurant.

To illustrate his methods, Jacky selects a Beef Wellington. A traditional dish of almost numbing familiarity in uninspired hands, it acquires renewed vigor when Jacky slices off the bottom to reduce the amount of soggy crust and, as a substitute for the usual sauce Perigueux, presents two sauces, a coulis of truffles and a beure blanc.

He uses the term *nouvelle cuisine*, but his is a very careful definition. He speaks primarily of remodeling classical ideas. "Cooking is international now. We take ideas from many places. You cannot talk about one style of cooking. The important thing is that cooking is an art, like music or painting, and cooks need to contribute something to the evolution of the customer's taste."

Jacky came to Ernie's in 1976 following work as a chef in Florida and in Boston. Before moving to the United States, he worked at Maxim's and Prunier in Paris. Jacky's decision to become a cook was dictated by economic necessity, and it was not until ten years ago that he really began to love the work.

At Ernie's he has found a restaurant suited to his interest in melding the traditional and the contemporary. Ernie's has been a San Francisco institution for several decades. Set between the old Italian neighborhood of North Beach and San Francisco's bustling Financial District, Ernie's bridges the old and the new San Francisco.

From its brass name plate to its two spacious dining rooms, Ernie's is lavishly baroque. Walls are covered with red silk brocade, matched by burgundy carpets and burgundy velvet chairs. Ornate chandeliers, a long carved bar, and private dining rooms recreate the atmosphere of San Francisco at the turn of the century. Framed prints from a 1905 magazine portray winsome ladies and hopeful gentlemen. Antiques from old San Francisco abound, as do large floral arrangements and European waiters.

Although Ernie's is capable of seating 120 people, Jacky retains close control over the kitchen. He makes all the sauces and specials, and he adds the final touch to each plate leaving the kitchen. In addition to his creative entrées and hors d'oeuvres, Jacky places particular emphasis upon the desserts, many of which are made to order.

In noting the influences that have shaped his cooking, Jacky mentions first his childhood home in Normandy. "I was born with cows and apple trees around my house, so dairy products are very important to me." He is also a student of oriental cooking, an enthusiasm nurtured by his Korean wife.

Terms such as *beauty* and *good taste* help Jacky define the scope of his commitment to cooking. He seeks, not to startle with outrageous interpretations, but to be absorbed in the flow of culinary tradition, to take inspiration from the great chefs of the past and to refine their work, clarifying and molding it to match the concerns of today's diners. ✗

ERNIE'S
SAN FRANCISCO

MENU

SHRIMP-STUFFED RAVIOLI WITH BASIL SAUCE
Fresh pasta with shrimp stuffing, topped with a cream and fresh basil sauce

BRAISED SQUAB IN A MOLD OF VEGETABLES
Squab, cabbage, and fresh vegetables baked in a mold, then served with squab sauce

GRATIN OF STRAWBERRIES
Molded fresh strawberries on génoise cake topped with pastry cream and a sugar glaze

✗

SHRIMP-STUFFED
RAVIOLI WITH BASIL
SAUCE

SERVINGS: 4
PREPARATION: 1 HOUR

FILLING
2 tablespoons butter
1 onion, finely chopped
1 garlic clove, finely chopped
4 tomatoes, skinned, seeded and
  coarsely chopped
½ pound fresh shrimp, peeled,
  deveined, and finely chopped

Melt butter in sauté pan, then cook onion and garlic in butter for a few minutes. Add tomatoes and shrimp, then simmer for 15 minutes. Add cayenne pepper, salt, and white pepper, then cook for 35 minutes. Place in refrigerator until cold.

PASTA
9 ounces flour
1 egg
1 tablespoon unsalted butter, melted
¼ cup water
1 teaspoon salt
egg wash (1 egg, dash of olive oil, salt
  and pepper)

In a mixing bowl, combine flour and egg. Mix slowly, adding cooled melted butter, water, and salt. Mix only enough to incorporate, then run through pasta machine to form thin sheets.

SAUCE
½ cup fresh basil purée (in blender, add
  fresh basil to 1 tablespoon white
  wine)
2 cups heavy cream
2 tablespoons Parmesan cheese, grated
salt and white pepper to taste

Reduce basil purée by one-half. Add cream, reduce to a smooth consistency, and remove from heat. Add Parmesan cheese, salt and white pepper. Strain and reserve. (Sauce should be of a medium consistency.)

42

ASSEMBLY

Lay buttered sheet of parchment paper on work surface. On parchment, place one sheet of pasta and brush with egg wash. Place a large spoonful of filling about every 4 inches on pasta sheet. Lay second sheet of pasta over the top and form tightly around filling, then brush with egg wash. Cut around piles of filling and parchment to form raviolis. Place raviolis in sauté pan, and cover with water. Bring to a boil and cook *al dente*. Place cooked ravioli on plate and cover with sauce. Garnish with fresh basil leaves and chopped tomato.

SERVINGS: 4
PREPARATION TIME: 2 HOURS

BRAISED SQUAB IN A
MOLD OF
VEGETABLES

SQUABS AND SAUCE
4 *squabs, wings and neck off and reserved*
salt and pepper
1 *pound butter, clarified*
1 *onion, chopped*
4 *slices of bacon, diced*
4 *small or two large cabbages, quartered and sliced (discard cores)*
½ *quart veal stock, thickened with cornstarch*

Brown pigeon wings and neck in oven and reserve. Salt and pepper inside and outside of squab. In large sauté pan, heat butter (do not use too much butter or birds will deep fry). Add squabs and brown on every side. Place birds in warm spot. Discard used butter in pan, add four tablespoons new clarified butter. Add bacon and onions, sauté to blond color. Add cabbages. Cook over low heat for twenty minutes, stirring occasionally. Add veal stock to cover and adjust seasoning. Bring to a boil. Place squabs on cabbage in sauté pan, brush with clarified butter, and cook in a 450-degree oven for 10 minutes. Remove squabs from the pan, bone them and put bones in saucepan with previously cut wings and necks. Reserve squab meat. Into saucepan with bones, strain the juice from the cabbage mixture. Add veal stock if liquid is needed. Reserve the cabbage. Over medium

(continued)

Braised Squab in a Mold of Vegetables

heat, cook the strained cabbage juice and bones for at least one-half hour, then strain through chinois and reserve sauce.

VEGETABLES AND MOLDS
3 pounds large turnips, peeled
2 pounds large carrots, peeled
1 broccoli flower per mold
salt

Cook carrots, turnips, and broccoli in heavily salted water until crisp. Cool vegetables in bowl placed in ice water. Select largest turnip, slice at its widest part into 4 slices, about ⅛-inch thick and about 3½ inches in diameter. In the middle of each of these turnip slices, cut a round hole about 1 inch in diameter. Cut remaining turnips and carrots into 40 rectangular slices about 1½ inch by 1 inch by ⅛ inch. On the bottom of 4 buttered 4-inch soufflé molds, place one each of the large turnip slices. Arrange the remaining vegetables slices around the inside edge of the molds, alternating carrot and turnip slices. Place a broccoli flower, stem off and head down, into the hole in the large turnip slices at the bottom of each mold. Cover with one layer of cabbage packed around broccoli and vegetables. Top cabbage layer with squab meat. Add more cabbage, pressing hard to form the mixture at top of mold. In a small sheet pan, place molded squabs with water around them and buttered parchment paper on each mold. Reheat for 20 minutes. (Note: If molds are not to be cooked until a later time, they should remain in oven about 20 minutes on low heat.) Unmold on serving plates. Spoon warmed sauce around molds and serve.

SERVINGS: 10
PREPARATION TIME: 1 HOUR

GRATIN OF
STRAWBERRIES

1 cup fresh large strawberries
génoise
    4 ounces sugar
    5 ounces water
    8 egg whites
10 ounces pastry cream
        5 oz regular cream plus
        5 oz regular cream mixed with 2 oz
        fresh squeezed lemon juice
⅓ ounce gelatin
crème anglaise (see page 9)
strawberry purée

Remove stems from strawberries and slice in half. Slice génoise into very thin pieces to fit in bottom of 10 molds, 3–4 inches in diameter. (For molds, use plastic pipe cut into 2-inch strips.) Line molds with sliced strawberries, cut side facing outward. In a saucepan, heat the sugar and water to a 250-degree softball. Meanwhile, place egg whites in bowl of mixer and whip to medium peaks. In metal bowl, whip together pastry creams over boiling water. When cream is quite hot, take off heat, slowly dissolve powdered gelatin in cream. When softball of sugar is formed, add to egg whites while still whipping on mixer. Continue whipping until firm. (As the sugar cools, a meringue will form.) Add this cream to the pastry creams then spoon the mixture into center of molds. Chill at least one hour. To serve, unmold and sprinkle tops of molds with a tiny bit of sugar. Glaze under broiler and unmold on serving plates. Serve with crème anglaise and strawberry purée.

CHEF CHRISTIAN ISER
FOURNOU'S OVENS

Christian Iser, the executive chef at San Francisco's Stanford Court Hotel, is a professional familiar with the highest standards of service and cuisine. To achieve that knowledge, he had first to defy his family, who considered him a black sheep because of his insistence upon training as a chef. He was at last permitted to leave his birthplace in Cognac, France to attend cooking school in Paris.

After three years' apprenticeship, he served in the French Navy and later on several luxury liners sailing between Eu-

rope and the United States. As he enjoyed his visits to this country, it was natural that he eventually take a position as chef in a small East Coast restaurant. When he came to love California, his move to San Francisco and to the Stanford Court in 1974 was inevitable.

Christian is a dark, intense man who is extremely proud of the Stanford Court's kitchen staff and who is pleased with his work in this large hotel. He finds that the clientele is generally receptive to fine cuisine and also interested in sampling new foods. And since his speciality is garnishing and decoration, the hotel provides the chance to practice those arts. "I enjoy very much the opportunity to do banquets and to make the ice carvings and decorations. In a restaurant, there is no time for that."

In San Francisco, large hotels do not generally boast good restaurants, but hotel president James Nassikas is determined that his will be an exception. An example of his efforts are the private dining rooms on the restaurant's upper level. Access to those rooms is through a hallway lined with small, locked storage bins, each bearing the name of a regular Stanford Court customer and each containing the private wines reserved for that guest's next visit.

The restaurant has a separate entrance leading into a large bar and cocktail area with views of downtown San Francisco and the cable cars climbing Nob Hill. A series of tiered dining areas step down from the bar to the restaurant's focal point, the ovens.

A terra cotta floor, burnished copper cookware, and artful lighting heighten the ovens' dramatic setting. They are used for roast and steaks and are wood-fired, but Christian admits they also use gas to maintain even heat.

Given the size of the Stanford Court's food operation, it is not surprising that the menu at Fournou's Ovens is somewhat traditional. In addition to meats from the ovens, guests may also order crab, several types of fish, and assorted styles of veal prepared in the large, well-equipped kitchen.

Desserts are another specialty at Fournou's Ovens. Pastry chef Jim Dodge grew up in a family of hotel owners and always wanted to have his own hotel. Instead, while living in New Hampshire, he learned the intricacies of baking in a Swiss pastry shop. After a series of jobs in hotels throughout the United States, he came to the Stanford Court in 1978.

Extremely serious about his work, Jim explains that the kitchen uses about 100 pounds of flour each day to make pastas, breads, and crusts; about 100 pounds of sugar is needed daily for the desserts, sorbets, and syrups. His range of experience has given Jim a fine sense of the different styles of baking. "The Europeans tend to blend many flavors in one dessert. The Americans are simpler, having fewer flavors and depending upon superior products."

Christian and Jim are representatives of the best in hotel chefs. Over the years, their efforts at the Stanford Court and Fournou's Ovens have brought praise from critics and, more telling, patronage from local diners. ✄

FOURNOU'S OVENS
STANFORD COURT HOTEL, SAN FRANCISCO

47

FOURNOU'S OVENS

MENU

CASSOLETTE OF LANGOUSTINE

Imported langoustine lobster and scallops sautéed, then served with a white vermouth and cream sauce

RACK OF LAMB WITH HERB SAUCE

Rack of lamb marinated in oil and herbs, roasted, and served with a rich ham, pickle, mushroom, and mint sauce

SALAD

Lettuce, endive, shrimp, and Roquefort cheese mixed in a mustard vinaigrette

STANFORD COURT BREAD PUDDING

Brioche and raspberries with custard, baked, and topped with powdered sugar

CINNAMON PEACH TART

Cinnamon dough tart filled with fresh peaches and brushed with apricot glaze

SERVINGS: 4
PREPARATION TIME: 1 HOUR

12 langoustine
 4 scallops
 2 tablespoons olive oil
 2 tablespoons butter
 2 tablespoons shallots, finely chopped
 2 teaspoons lemon juice
¼ cup white vermouth
 1 cup heavy cream
 2 teaspoons fish velouté (fish stock,
    roux, salt, and pepper)
 1 medium carrot, julienned
 1 leek, julienned
 1 celery stalk, julienned
salt and pepper

Shell langoustine. Soak scallops in cold running water to clean. In sauté pan, heat oil and butter, then sauté shallots. Add langoustine, salt, pepper, and scallops. Sauté quickly, underdone; remove langoustine and scallops with slotted spoon and drain. Deglaze with lemon juice and vermouth. Add cream, fish velouté, salt and pepper and cook until sauce is thick and smooth, whisking occasionally. Add julienned vegetables, langoustine, and scallops and cook very briefly. On individual serving plates, dish out three langoustine and one scallop. Pour sauce and julienned vegetables over top and garnish with chopped parsley.

SERVINGS: 4
PREPARATION TIME: 1½ HOURS (NOTE ELAPSED TIME)

MARINADE
 4 carrots
 2 celery stalks
 3 onions
 2 bunches thyme
10 bay leaves
 1 bunch rosemary
 1 bunch parsley
 4 garlic cloves, unpeeled
 1 tablespoon whole black pepper
 2 cups salad oil

Dice carrot, celery, and onion. Coarsely chop thyme, bay leaves, rosemary, parsley, and garlic. Add salad oil and mix all ingredients together in a large bowl. Rub over rack of lamb and marinate for 48 hours, turning occasionally.

(continued)

LAMB

marinade

    2 racks of lamb
    2 lamb bones
    8 large mushrooms, (6 chopped whole for sauce and 2 tops only, julienned)
    2 bunches fresh mint
1½ cups red wine
    2 quarts demi-glace (lamb or veal)
bouquet garni—thyme, rosemary, parsley, bay leaf
    4 ounces cooked ham, julienned
    1 large dill pickle, julienned
    4 ounces butter
    2 medium carrots
    1 cup snow peas
    1 tablespoon sugar
salt and pepper to taste
watercress for garnish

Remove lamb from marinade and drain. Strain vegetables in marinade and reserve. In large roasting pan, brown lamb bones at 500 degrees for 15 minutes. Add drained mirepoix from marinade and brown another five minutes. Strain contents of roasting pan to eliminate fat and then transfer bones and vegetables to stock pot. Add 6 chopped mushrooms and mint, then deglaze roasting pan with red wine. Add demi-glace and bouquet garni and cook for two hours, skimming carefully and adjusting seasoning. Strain this sauce through chinois into pan. Heat sauce. Add julienned ham, pickle, and 2 mushroom tops to sauce and adjust seasoning. Salt and pepper racks of lamb and sprinkle with thyme. Put racks of lamb in a roasting pan and roast for 15–18 minutes. Remove rack from roasting pan and let racks rest for five minutes before carving. Blanch carrots and snow peas, then sauté in butter and reserve. (Season snow peas with salt, sugar, and black pepper.) Cut racks in half, four ribs per person. Warm sauce and ladle around racks. Garnish with sautéed carrots, snow peas, and watercress.

50

SERVINGS: 4
PREPARATION TIME: 15 MINUTES

DRESSING
 1 cup salad oil
 ¼ cup red tarragon vinegar
 1 egg yolk
 1 tablespoon Dijon mustard

SALAD
 1 head butter lettuce
 1 head endive
 2 ounces small shrimp ("Bay Shrimp")
 2 ounces Roquefort cheese, crumbled
 1 bay Enoki mushrooms
 parsley, chopped
 salt and ground pepper

Mix egg yolk and mustard with whip, add vinegar, then slowly pour in salad oil while whipping. Salt and pepper to taste.

Wash lettuce and endive. Toss lettuce with dressing, sprinkle with coarse ground pepper, 3 leaves on each serving plate. Julienne endive and toss with dressing; then sprinkle on lettuce. Toss shrimp with dressing and sprinkle on lettuce. Sprinkle with Roquefort cheese, mushrooms, and parsley and serve.

SERVINGS: 12
PREPARATION TIME: 1 HOUR (NOTE ELAPSED TIME)

STANFORD COURT
BREAD PUDDING

BRIOCHE
 1 pound bread flour
 1½ ounces sugar
 ½ ounce fresh active (cake or
   compressed) yeast
 ½ ounce salt
 5 eggs
 8 ounces room temperature
   unsalted butter

In bowl mix flour, sugar and yeast. Blend well then add salt. Add eggs and continue mixing until dough is smooth. Add butter in 4 stages, working each piece into dough before adding more. Continue mixing until dough is very elastic and clings to spoon. Cover with plastic wrap and chill six hours. Unwrap dough and cut in half. Shape each half into a ball and then work into a loaf with the palm of the hand. Place each loaf into a clean loaf pan and let stand in warm spot (see note below). When the dough has become slightly puffy, deflate with hands. Allow dough to rise again, to the top of the pan. Bake in preheated 350-degree oven about 45 minutes, until dough pulls away from the sides of the pan and is golden brown. Turn loaves out of pans and let cool on wire rack. Only one loaf is used in Bread Pudding.

Note: Brioche is a very slow rising bread. It must rise in a warm place (75 to 80 degrees) that is free of drafts for about 4 to 5 hours.

(continued)

51

Stanford Court Bread Pudding

FRUIT AND CUSTARD
  2 *medium green apples*
  1 *pint raspberries or sliced strawberries*
  6 *eggs*
  1 *cup sugar*
  ½ *cup flour*
  1 *quart heavy cream*

Mix the eggs, sugar, and flour together until smooth. Pour in the cream and blend well. Peel, core, and slice apples. Cut crust off brioche, slice, then cut into triangles.

Butter a 2½ quart soufflé dish and line bottom with one-third of brioche slices. Cover brioche with apple slices, then add one-third of custard over apples. Form second layer of brioche slices and cover with layer of raspberries (sliced strawberries may be substituted). Pour another one-third of custard over raspberries. Top with remaining brioche and custard. Bake at 375 degrees for 60-70 minutes or until top is golden brown and custard slightly firm. Sprinkle with powdered sugar and serve when completely cool.

SERVINGS: 12
PREPARATION TIME: 1¼ HOURS

CINNAMON DOUGH
2½ cups all-purpose flour
¾ cup sugar
5 ounces butter
2 tablespoons ground cinnamon
¼ teaspoon baking powder
¼ cup cold water

Form a large ring of flour on work surface. In the center of the ring of flour make a mound of sugar, baking powder, and cinnamon; also make a mound of butter cut into small squares. With palm of hand, cream butter and add to the sugar mixture while continuing to cream. Push flour into center and blend with butter/sugar mixture into a coarse meal. Add all the water, press to mix in water, then work into ball with palms to an equal consistency having no dry spots. Roll out one 10-inch tart shell on floured work surface. Chill about half an hour. Mold aluminum foil in pan and bake in 350-degree preheated oven 15–20 minutes until golden brown.

APRICOT GLAZE
1 cup apricot jam
½ cup sugar
¼ cup water

Combine jam, sugar and water in heavy saucepan. Mix well, bring to a boil, then simmer until clear.

PEACH FILLING
8–10 very ripe peaches
1½ cups apricot glaze

Cut each peach into eight sections and arrange snugly in baked tart shell. Lightly brush apricot glaze over all peaches and serve.

*Pastry chef Jim Dodge prepares
Cinnamon Peach Tart*

CHEF BARBARA TROPP
CHINA MOON

*F*ood writer and cooking instructor Barbara Tropp defines the basis of Chinese cuisine: "The idea of yin and yang is fundamental. Anyone who wants to be a Chinese cook must have an understanding of that." The yin-yang concept is one of thoroughgoing contrast, of harmony, of coordinated opposites. It represents, above all, dynamic balance.

As a New Jersey schoolgirl Barbara was never particularly interested in food, but did become fascinated by Chinese culture and eventually moved to Taiwan for two years to study art and history. Although she was there as a student in the university, her real education came under Po-Fu, a seventy-year-old gourmand who introduced her to the subtleties of Chinese cuisine. "We began eating each morning in his home. Then we would go to the markets—squeezing chickens, poking fish, haggling with the merchants."

From those years, Barbara learned that in China to be civilized is to understand the buying, preparation, and enjoyment of food. Upon her return to the United States, she began to cook in order to recapture the taste memories of the Orient. "I had to learn the techniques and from the techniques I got back to the tastes."

Her involvement with China was so consuming that she wrote what many critics consider to be the definitive Chinese cookbook. Published in 1982, *The Modern Art of Chinese Cooking* explains in words and illustrations the basics of Chinese culinary methods. It is the theoretical foundation of Barbara's own cooking.

In the book she reminds readers that Chinese cuisine is no less diverse than is the cooking of Italy or France. China is a huge country that deserves careful, regional study. She also emphasizes the melding of Chinese and Western cooking philosophies. Thus she endorses the extensive use of wine and often provides recipes for European tarts and sorbets.

To give life to her thought, Barbara will open her own restaurant in 1984. China Moon will be a bistro featuring Chinese food, European and California wines, and French-style desserts.

Western chefs often admit to being influenced by oriental cooking, but few have the training or the skills to fuse Western technique and Eastern philosophy. Barbara emphatically believes such a combination is not only possible, but also necessary. Her roll in China Moon will be that of a teacher rather than a working chef.

Yin and yang are at work here. Barbara knows that most Chinese restaurants in the United States offer what they believe the customer expects. "In fact, real Chinese cooking is either done at home very simply or in restaurants that are very fancy."

She remarks that, because China has always considered itself to be the central player in all of history, it does not readily adopt ideas from other countries. Barbara's talent is her ability to apply new tenets in California cooking to old concepts in Chinese cuisine.

Her book, her cooking lessons, and her new restaurant are expressions of her desire to share the wonders of Chinese food. Like the Chinese, her methods are based upon freshness, simplicity, and clarity of taste. She is unhappy that the essence of Chinese cooking is often denied Americans. "Most people have only tasted canned water chestnuts. One of the reasons for opening China Moon is to use fresh water chestnuts."

A small, impeccably dressed woman, Barbara speaks wistfully of the delights she experienced in Taiwan. That sojourn is recreated each time she cooks. In her delicate handling of the food is a reverence for Chinese tradition and history. For her, Chinese food is a comfort and an aid in recalling her joyful memories of China. ✗

CHINA MOON
SAN FRANCISCO

Yin-Yang Raspberry and Mandarin Orange Tart

55

MENU

STEAMED SHAO-MAI DUMPLINGS WITH YOUNG GINGER
Small steamed dumplings stuffed with fresh water chestnuts, pork, and scallions

SHRIMP AND CRAB TOAST ON FRENCH BAGUETTES WITH FRESH PLUM SAUCE
Baguette slices topped with shrimp and crab, deep-fried, then served with plum sauce

TEA AND CASSIA BARK SMOKED CHICKEN WITH HUNAN RED ONION PICKLE GARNISH
Whole chicken rubbed with Szechuan peppercorns, steamed, smoked, cut into pieces, and served with cucumber fans

MA-LA CUCUMBER FANS
Garnish for smoked chicken

PAN-FRIED NOODLE PILLOW WITH STIR-FRIED CHINESE GREENS AND BABY GARLIC
Noodle cushion browned, then served with stir-fried vegetables

YIN-YANG RASPBERRY AND MANDARIN ORANGE TART
Raspberry and orange tart brushed with passion fruit glaze

✗

SERVINGS: 4–6
PREPARATION TIME: 45 MINUTES

16 *paper-thin shao-mai wrappers
    (purchased from a Chinese grocery;
    stamped out of thin won-ton
    wrappers with a 3-inch cookie cutter
    or rolled out with a pasta machine)*
 1 *walnut-sized nugget young ginger*
 1 *thin scallion, cut into 1-inch lengths*
½ *pound ground pork butt*
 1 *tablespoon soy sauce*
 2 *teaspoons Chinese rice wine or dry
    sherry*
 1 *teaspoon Chinese or Japanese sesame
    oil*
¼ *teaspoon kosher salt*
ground pepper to taste
¼ *cup diced fresh water chestnuts*
 3 *tablespoons diced carrots*

Mince ginger and scallion in food processor until fine. Add pork, soy sauce, wine, sesame oil, salt and pepper and mix with on-off turns in processor. Scrape mixture into bowl, add water chestnuts, then stir in one direction until mixed.

Put 1 scant tablespoon filling in center of wrapper. Form wrapper into a loose four-cornered hat, then press each corner towards filling. Dumpling now looks like a cupcake. Next, make a circle of your thumb and first finger around the middle of the dumpling and tighten the circle gently to press the wrapper to the filling and give the dumpling an empire "waist." Dunk exposed pork top into carrot cubes to decorate. Steam dumplings 20 minutes on an oiled steamer rack and serve.

SERVINGS: 4
PREPARATION TIME: 30 MINUTES

12 *diagonally-cut slices French
    baguette, a scant ¾-inch thick*
¼ *pound fresh shrimp, shelled and
    deveined*
¼ *pound fresh crabmeat*
 1 *tablespoon finely minced fresh
    ginger*
 1 *tablespoon finely minced scallion,
    white and light green parts only*
 1 *tablespoon minced fresh lard*
1½ *teaspoons kosher salt*
 2 *teaspoons Chinese rice wine or dry
    sherry*
 2 *teaspoons water*
 4 *teaspoons cornstarch*
¼ *cup diced fresh waterchestnuts*
 1 *egg white, stiffly beaten*

Leave baguette slices out on a rack overnight to dry, or place in a low oven for about 10 minutes per side until dry to the touch. Mince shrimp and crabmeat to a paste, then combine with the remaining ingredients, stirring well in one direction to blend. Fold in beaten egg white.

(continued)

57

ASSEMBLY
black sesame seeds
minced Smithfield ham
fresh whole coriander leaves
corn or peanut oil for deep-frying
sauce made from puréed soft plums
  simmered with sugar, rice vinegar
  and plum wine to taste

Using a broad-bladed sandwich spreader, mound shrimp on bread slice to a thickness of a scant ¾ inch, tapering mound where it meets the edge of the bread to form a smooth dome. Sprinkle sesame seeds and ham bits thinly on top, then press on a single coriander leaf. Deep-fry, topping side down, in 350-degree oil until topping is golden, about 4 minutes. Using long cooking chopsticks or tongs, turn toasts to brown the underside of the baguette. Remove promptly to paper towels to drain. Serve with warm or cooled plum sauce.

TEA AND CASSIA BARK SMOKED CHICKEN WITH HUNAN RED ONION PICKLE GARNISH

SERVINGS: 4
PREPARATION TIME: 2 HOURS (SEE ELAPSED TIME)

3½–4 pound chicken, fresh killed
2½ tablespoons kosher salt
  1 tablespoon Szechuan brown peppercorns
  ½ teaspoon finely minced fresh ginger
2 teaspoons finely minced fresh orange peel
  2 medium whole scallions, cut into 3 inch lengths
4 quarter-size slices fresh ginger
¼ cup dry lichee black tea leaves
  ⅓ cup packed brown sugar
  ⅓ cup raw rice
  1 tablespoon Szechwan brown peppercorns
  3 whole star anise (or 24 individual points)
  ⅛ cup crumbled cassia bark
5-7 finger lengths home-dried orange peel (To make, remove peel from fresh oranges and allow to dry on counter until curled.)
1-1½ teaspoons Chinese or Japanese sesame oil

Remove kidneys nestled to either side of chicken tail bone, then flush chicken with cold water inside and out and pat dry. Heat salt and peppercorns in a dry skillet over medium-low heat, stirring constantly, until salt turns off-white and peppercorns are very fragrant, about 3 minutes. Grind hot mixture to a powder in a food processor or mortar, then sieve to remove peppercorn husks. Rub pepper-salt, ginger, and orange peel over outside and inside of chicken. Put chicken breast-side up in a heatproof pie plate, cover with plastic film, and set aside 24 hours at room temperature or up to 48 hours in the refrigerator. Drain marinating juices. Smash scallion lengths and ginger coins to release juices, then array on top of chicken and in cavity. Steam 30 minutes over medium-high heat. Let rest in steamer additional 5 minutes before removing lid. Drain

(continued)

58

steaming juices. (These can be strained, chilled, and used to make sauces and season soups and stir-frys.) Remove scallion and ginger. Line old wok and lid with super heavy-duty tin foil. Combine tea, sugar, rice, peppercorns, anise, cassia bark and dried orange peel, and scatter in bottom of lined wok. Place chicken breast side up on oiled smoking rack in wok set above spices. Turn heat to high, wait until smoke sends up several thick plumes, then cover wok and crimp foil shut to contain smoke. Smoke chicken over medium-high heat, for 12 minutes, then turn off heat and let chicken rest in sealed wok for 7 minutes. Remove bird, brush with sesame oil, then chop into pieces with a thick-bladed cleaver designed to cut through bones. Garnish smoked chicken with Hunan Red Onion Pickles. Use Ma-La Cucumber Fans as side dish. (see page 60)

GARNISH

½ *pound very firm red onions*
6½ *tablespoons unseasoned Japanese rice vinegar*
3–3½ *tablespoons sugar*
⅛ *teaspoon dried red chili flakes*
⅛ *teaspoon Szechwan brown peppercorns*
2–3 *large cloves garlic, lightly smashed, then peeled*

Remove tips and peel of onions. Cut evenly into rings ⅜ inch thick. Separate rings, removing any loose inner membranes. Combine vinegar, 3 tablespoons sugar, chili, peppercorns, and garlic in a heavy, non-aluminum saucepan. Stir over moderate heat to dissolve sugar, then simmer three minutes. Taste and adjust if needed with remaining sugar to balance sweet, tart, and spicy flavors. Add onion rings, then toss with chopsticks until onion wilts and liquid regains simmer, three to four minutes. Scrape mixture into a shallow bowl and refrigerate. Before serving, remove any loose onion membranes and most of the peppercorns.

½ pound firm Japanese or Kirby
  cucumbers
1 teaspoon kosher salt
1½ teaspoons corn or peanut oil
1 teaspoon fresh ginger, thinly cut
1½ teaspoons finely minced fresh garlic
scant ¼ teaspoon dried red chili flakes
¼ teaspoon Szechwan brown
  peppercorns
½ teaspoon soy sauce
1 tablespoon unseasoned Japanese rice
  vinegar
1½ tablespoons sugar
1 teaspoon sesame oil

Remove tips from cucumbers, then cut cucumbers into 2-inch lengths. Grasp cucumber lengthwise between chopsticks held in a V-shape on cutting board, then cut cucumber crosswise at ⅛-inch intervals into a fan (chopsticks prevent knife from cutting clear through cucumber). Toss cucumbers with salt and set aside for thirty minutes to soften. Drain, rinse with cold water, then press gently between palms to remove excess water. Heat a wok or medium-size heavy skillet over moderate heat until hot enough to sizzle a bead of water slowly. Add corn or peanut oil, swirl to glaze bottom, then reduce heat to low. When hot enough to sizzle a ginger thread, add ginger, garlic, chili, and peppercorns. Toss until fully fragrant, about ten seconds, then add a pinch more chili if your nose tells you it's needed. Add cucumber, toss to combine, then add soy, vinegar, sugar and sesame oil. Toss until sugar dissolves and liquid is hot. Taste and adjust with a bit more sugar if needed to bring out the full flavor of the chili. Scrape mixture into a shallow bowl and set aside to cool, stirring occasionally. Before serving, remove most of the peppercorns.

Pan-Fried Noodle Pillow with Stir-Fried Chinese Greens and Baby Garlic

SERVINGS: 4
PREPARATION TIME: 25 MINUTES

NOODLE PILLOW

½ *pound* ¹⁄₁₆-*inch thin fresh Chinese
 egg noodles*
2 *teaspoons Chinese or Japanese sesame
 oil*
1 *teaspoon kosher salt*
5–6 *tablespoons corn or peanut oil*
black sesame seeds, to garnish

Boil noodles in unsalted water until
al dente. Drain, flush with cold
water until chilled, then roll loosely
in a lint-free towel to blot off excess
water. Toss noodles with sesame
oil and salt, using your hands to
coat and separate the strands. Heat
a 12-inch well-seasoned or Silver-
stone heavy skillet over high heat
until hot enough to evaporate a
bead of water on contact. Add 5
tablespoons oil, swirl to coat bottom
and sides of pan, then reduce heat
to medium-high. When oil is hot
enough to sizzle a single noodle,
coil noodles in pan then use spatula
to pack them into an even pancake
or "pillow." Cover and cook until
bottom is golden, about 5–7 minutes. Uncover, flip pillow over with
a jerk of your wrist, then cover and
cook second side. If pan seems dry,

(continued)

61

dribble in the remaining tablespoon of oil around the side of the skillet before covering it. Slide noodle pillow out of pan, cut into quarters, then garnish with a sprinkling of black sesame seeds.

Soak dried mushrooms several hours or overnight in cold water. Drain, rinse, remove stems, then cut caps into slivers ⅛-inch wide. Heat wok or large heavy skillet over high heat until hot enough to evaporate a bead of water on contact. Add 2 tablespoons oil, swirl to glaze pan, then reduce heat to medium-high. Add chinese chive tops, garlic and black mushrooms, toss until fully fragrant, then add chanterelles, mustard greens and cabbage to pan. Toss just until vegetables turn supple, about 2 minutes. Add baby bok choy and chinese cabbage, toss until color deepens and the vegetables are heated through, about 20 seconds. If the pan becomes too dry, dribble in a bit more oil from the side. Fold in chilies, then turn contents onto serving plate, either alongside or on top of noodle pillow. Caution: Chilies are added for color and are not meant to be eaten whole! If spicy dish is wanted, finely sliver a single chili and stir-fry with shallots before stir-frying remaining vegetables.

STIR-FRIED GREENS

1 tablespoon Chinese chives
⅛ cup finely sliced baby garlic
6 medium-sized Chinese dried black mushrooms
1½ cups sliced chanterelles
1½ teaspoons finely sliced mustard greens
3 cups sliced baby bok choy, flower-like bases left whole
2 cups Chinese cabbage, sliced
several small fresh red and orange chilies
2–3 tablespoons corn or peanut oil

YIN-YANG
RASPBERRY AND
MANDARIN ORANGE
TART

1 *partially baked 9-inch tart shell*
⅓ *cup sugar*
4 *tablespoons sweet butter, cubed*
4 *ounces almond paste*
2 *large eggs*
2 *teaspoons Mandarin orange liqueur*
¼ *teaspoon orange flower water*
1 *pint fresh raspberries*
1–1½ *cups mandarin orange segments*
½ *cup passion fruit jam, melted*

Cream the sugar, butter and almond paste in a food processor. Add 1 egg, process to combine, then add the second egg and process until smooth. Add the liqueur and flower water, then process to blend. Pour the mixture into the partially baked shell. Bake 25–30 minutes in the center of a preheated 350-degree oven until the top is evenly browned and puffed. Remove the tart to a rack to cool. Arrange the raspberries and mandarin orange segments in a yin-yang pattern on top of the cooled filling. Brush the warm glaze thinly but evenly on top of the fruit and along the edge of the tart shell. Remove the rim of the tart pan before serving by centering the tart on your hand or a can.

CHEF UDO NECHUTNYS
THE MIRAMONTE RESTAURANT

Within the stone walls of an old hotel situated in a small town in California's Napa Valley, Udo Nechutnys and his partner Edouard Platel built Miramonte, an appealing showcase for Udo's culinary talents. The restaurant features a formal dining room, a cool patio shaded by a 100-year-old fig tree, and a quiet tavern, its walls festooned with antique farming tools and photographs of California winemakers.

A German by birth, Udo—as he is known by everyone—decided at age seven to be a chef. At seventeen he was apprenticed to a teacher in Barbizon, France, where he mastered the intricate fundamentals of French cooking. After his training, Udo spent a year at Maxim's in Paris.

Then, under the tutelage of Paul Bocuse in Lyon, Udo was given the chance to work at the Mandarin in Hong Kong. There he met his Chinese-American wife and remained for two years. Following a brief stay in Lyon, he returned to the Orient to teach at Japan's foremost culinary school. From Japan, again with the assistance of Bocuse, he came to California to oversee the restaurant at Domaine Chandon, Moet-Hennessey's new facility in the Napa Valley.

Now in his mid-thirties and master of his own restaurant, Udo reflects this blend of a precise, informed European technique and a disciplined, Oriental feeling for the origins and purposes of food. "The Orient taught me to enjoy food," he says, "to respect each tiny detail of its preparation."

Intense eyes dominate Udo's ascetic face, an image belied by his active, sensuous involvement with food. As he cooks, Udo's hands are in constant motion over, around, and in the food. He cooks by taste, smell, and sight. Above all, by touch. "A chef cannot cook without his fingers."

Diners at Miramonte are offered an intriguing menu. Udo's recipes mirror his belief that even the latest culinary trends are only evolutionary developments of time-honored principles. For him, today's cooking reflects people's concern with health and sports. His methods may remain essentially French, but the combination of foods and the presentation is innovative. Instead of a traditional mousse appetizer, he fashions small gateaux from chicken livers. His cooking wine is Cabernet Sauvignon, because he believes the wine should be of the same high quality as the other ingredients. Local products, such as figs from his own tree, are also featured in Udo's cooking.

He has been cooking for many years and still loves it, though the hours are long and demanding. "Sometimes, late at night, I hate cooking," he admits, "but in the morning I like it again."

Udo seldom ventures beyond his own home and Miramonte, preferring to create his recipes unhindered by fashion in the culinary world. Once each year he visits Europe or the Orient to rest and to renew friendships.

Contrasting the dining habits of Miramonte customers with those of other countries, he points out that "In Europe, to dine out is an experience. People want to relax. Here, they want to eat quickly and go home."

For a man intent upon creating an enchanting eating experience, this American attitude can be frustrating, but Udo is warmly appreciative of his reception in California. "We're in business to make money, of course, but my real pleasure is to satisfy the customer's belly. That is the hardest job." ✗

THE MIRAMONTE RESTAURANT
ST. HELENA, NAPA VALLEY

MENU

MOUSSE OF POULTRY LIVER
Individual chicken liver mousses presented in a fragrant tomato sauce

SALMON "IN MY STYLE"
Filleted salmon served over crayfish tails and green salad in a white wine and cream sauce

DUCK MIRAMONTE
Lightly baked breast of duck in a creamy sauce of its own stock and Cabernet Sauvignon

FIGS IN CABERNET SAUVIGNON WITH ALMOND ICE CREAM
Fresh fig halves marinated in Cabernet Sauvignon and served with Udo's vanilla ice cream

EGG SNOWBALL
Poached quenelles of egg white floating in a custardy Crème Anglaise and topped with fresh caramel sauce and toasted almonds

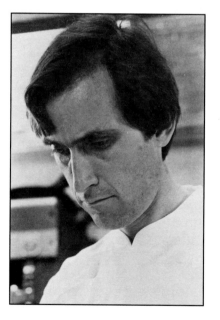

MOUSSE
½ onion, chopped
1 pound chicken livers
2 shallots
1 sprig thyme
2 garlic cloves
parsley
basil
3 eggs
7 ounces lard or duck fat
1 cup bread crumbs
1 cup heavy cream (amount may vary
    according to consistency)

Grind onion and livers in food grinder. Add shallots, thyme, garlic, parsley, and basil. Place processed mixture into bowl, add eggs, lard, bread crumbs (épice parisienne or cayenne pepper is optional), salt and pepper. Mix well. Put mixture into processor and blend until smooth. Add about 1 cup cream while blending. Pour back into bowl and adjust seasoning: (Note: mixture should be more liquid than thick—add more cream if needed.) Strain through chinois. Pour mixture into chilled, well-buttered ramekins. Put a layer of water in a sauté pan and place ramekins in pan. Cover ramekins with buttered parchment paper, then bring to a boil. Place in 450-degree oven for 8 minutes. Remove parchment and let set for 2 minutes.

TOMATO SAUCE
2 tablespoons olive oil
½ onion, chopped
2–3 garlic cloves, mashed
bouquet garni (parsley, bay leaf,
    oregano, thyme, rosemary)
1 cup water (actual amount may vary
    according to amount of juice in
    tomatoes)
flour
10 medium tomatoes

Heat olive oil in sauté pan. Add onion and garlic and cook until transparent. Add bouquet garni. Sprinkle onion mixture with flour to thicken sauce. Add tomatoes immediately and mix well. Reduce heat. Add 1 cup of water and cook 20–30 minutes. Salt and pepper to taste. Remove bouquet garni and put mixture into food processor and blend thoroughly (do not blend too much or color will change). Strain through chinois. May add 1 tablespoon butter for extra flavor if desired.

ASSEMBLY
chives
grated carrot
chervil
watercress
bay leaf

Unmold mousse onto serving plate. Spoon tomato sauce over mousse. Top with chopped chives, carrots, chervil, and watercress. Garnish with bay leaf.

67

FISH

2 pounds salmon fillet
2 tablespoons butter

Slice salmon from boned fish at angle, about 1–1½ inches thick. Pound thin under dampened plastic paper and store in parchment paper until ready to cook.

FISH FUMÉ

Fish bones (sole is best or use one-half
  salmon)
1–2 tablespoons butter
½ onion, sliced
½ carrot, sliced
bouquet garni (parsley, thyme, celery)
1½ cups white wine
1 cup chicken stock or water

Heat butter in saucepan. Add onions and carrot. Cook briefly, about 1 minute. Add fish bones (do not brown, but cook until meat falls off). Add bouquet garni, white wine and chicken stock or water. Bring to boil and cook 15 minutes. Remove bouquet garni. Strain through chinois. Reduce by half, strain again, and reserve.

WHITE WINE SAUCE

1–2 tablespoons butter
2–3 shallots, chopped
3 large mushrooms, chopped
1 cup white wine
reserved 2 cups fish fumé
1 cup heavy cream
salt and pepper

In sauté pan heat butter, then add shallots and mushrooms. Cook briefly. Add wine and fish fumé, cook about 5 minutes. Add cream to thicken (sauce should be more white than gray). Reduce for 20 minutes, then strain through chinois. Reduce for 3–4 more minutes. Sauce should be thick enough to coat a spoon. Whip, add salt and pepper and reserve.

SALAD

 6 crayfish tails
10 leaves spinach
 1 head endive
½ cup small green beans, blanched
 1 tomato, diced
 2 shallots, chopped
 1 bunch chervil, chopped
pinch tarragon
vinaigrette of hazelnut oil (1 part
  vinegar to 4 parts oil, mustard, salt
  and pepper to taste)
salt and pepper
10 leaves basil

Boil crayfish tails. Place spinach, endive, and blanched beans in a large bowl. Add tomato, shallots, chervil, and tarragon. Add crayfish tails and sprinkle with hazelnut oil, salt and pepper. Mix well.

ASSEMBLY

Salt salmon. In teflon pan, heat 2 tablespoons of butter. When butter is hot, take pan off heat, place salmon in pan, return pan to heat, and cook briefly. Remove from heat, turn once, and place back on heat. Take off heat and turn. To serve, spoon sauce into pool on plate, place salad in center of plate, and arrange salmon on salad. Garnish with red basil leaves.

SERVINGS: 4
PREPARATION TIME: 1 HOUR

DUCK MIRAMONTE

DUCK
4 breasts of duck
2 ounces butter
watercress
salt and pepper

Bone duck, reserving unused parts for stock. Trim breasts, salt and pepper well. In sauté pan, heat butter. Place breast skin side down to melt fat between the skin and meat. Brown lightly. Place in 450-degree oven for 8 minutes.

WINE SAUCE
4–6 ounces butter
5 shallots, unchopped
1 teaspoon peppercorns, cracked
5 ounces cépes, dry
½ bottle, Cabernet Sauvignon
1–1½ cups duck stock (jellied) or demi-glace
2 tomatoes, seeded and chopped, optional

In copper pan, melt 4 ounces butter and add shallots and peppercorns. Cook briefly. Add cépes and Cabernet Sauvignon. Reduce slightly. Add duck stock or demi-glace and tomatoes, if desired. Cook 20–30 minutes. Add butter if desired, whip, and reserve.

BONE MARROW
7 ounces bone marrow, chopped
salt

Fill saucepan with water and salt, then bring to a boil. Add marrow and cook about 5 minutes. Reserve.

SPINACH
1 bunch spinach
2 ounces butter
2–3 garlic cloves
pinch of nutmeg
salt and pepper

Blanch spinach in hot, salted water, then press slightly to dry. In sauté pan, heat butter until brown (buerre rosette-hazelnut in color). Add spinach, then nutmeg, salt and pepper. Cook about 20 seconds. Drain and reserve.

To serve, spoon wine sauce on serving plate. Add bone marrow to

(continued)

69

sauce. Trim bone from duck breasts and place breast skin side down and slice very thin. Fan duck slices on plate in sauce, garnish with watercress and spinach in side dish.

SERVINGS: 2
PREPARATION TIME: 30 MINUTES (NOTE ELAPSED TIME)

CRÈME ANGLAISE
1 quart milk
½ pound sugar
10–12 egg yolks, reserve whites
vanilla bean paste

In saucepan, bring milk to boil. Place sugar and egg yolks in mixer or bowl and whip well, then add vanilla bean paste. Add milk to sugar and eggs while whipping. Put this mixture into large metal bowl and heat slowly. Using wooden spatula, move egg yolks around so they will not cook. When puffed and mixed, cool by placing bowl in ice water.

FIGS
2 ripe figs
6 ounces Cabernet Sauvignon
sugar

Peel figs, cut in half and sprinkle tops with sugar. Place in flat bowl with Cabernet (or Port) and marinate overnight (at least 2–3 hours). Reserve figs and marinade.

ASSEMBLY
150 almonds, sliced and blanched
2 ounces pistachio paste

Pour Crème Anglaise into a saucepan, mix with 100 almonds and pistachio paste, then process in ice cream machine.

To serve, put figs on plate. Shape chilled Crème Anglaise into quenelles and add to plates. Pour marinade over figs, add whipped cream mixed with sugar. Sprinkle with almonds (chopped) and serve.

Egg Snowball

SERVINGS: 4
PREPARATION TIME: 45 MINUTES

QUENELLES
10 egg whites
1 vanilla bean
7 ounces sugar
1 quart water or milk

In large bowl, whip egg whites until very stiff. Add vanilla bean paste. Add sugar (amount of sugar varies—it must bind eggs). In large saucepan, heat (but do not boil) milk or water. Shape egg whites into quenelles and float in liquid to poach gently. After 2 minutes, turn with spoon dipped in cold water. Cook 3 more minutes, then remove to baking pan. Drain pan and briefly reserve quenelles.

CARAMEL
10 sugar cubes or 5 soupspoons sugar
5 soupspoons water

Boil sugar and water in saucepan until it forms caramel.

Scoop Crème Anglaise into serving bowl and then place quenelle in each bowl. Sprinkle with roasted almonds and top with caramel sauce. Garnish with fresh fruit of the season.

CHEF WERNER ALBRECHT
THE FRENCH ROOM, FOUR SEASONS CLIFT HOTEL

"*F*rance had excellent restaurants," notes Werner Albrecht, the Swiss chef at the Four Seasons Clift Hotel in San Francisco. "We had to compete somehow, so hotels became the major Swiss industry." The son of a farmer, Werner learned to love cooking in his mother's kitchen. Instead of taking over the family farm, he entered an apprenticeship in hotels and restaurants.

A sturdy man with a ready smile and an easy familiarity, Werner has spent most of his career in large hotels that offer him

scope for his imagination and encouragement for his interests. Following his training in Switzerland, he joined the Four Seasons chain in Toronto in 1974. He has worked for the company in Vancouver, Houston, and San Francisco, where he has run the kitchens of the Clift since 1982.

Born in 1951, Werner is young to be in charge of a major hotel kitchen, but his talent has insured that the Clift maintains its reputation for excellence. It is one of only eight hotels in the United States to be awarded the Mobil Travel Guide Five-Star rating. The Four Seasons management stress quality and service, and they are enlightened in their encouragement of individuality, allowing each chef wide latitude in overseeing each hotel food operation. As a result, every hotel and restaurant exhibits a distinctive character of its own.

Werner is quick to say that he usually works on the cooking line, not in his office. "I'm not really an executive chef; I'm a working chef. If I had my own restaurant, I wouldn't have the time to concentrate on the food."

At the Clift, he devotes most of his time to the creation and execution of menu ideas. Naturally, his freedom to experiment is limited by the policies of the parent company. The overriding consideration is for conservative rather than exotic cuisine. The food tends to be attractive and familiar, with entreés like sweetbreads, veal, roast tenderloin of beef, and duck.

But Werner also provides foods that match contemporary eating habits. His pasta roll is an example of this. "In California, pasta is 'in,' but there are so many different pastas. I was using sheets of pasta already for another dish, and I needed a pasta dish for lunch. I thought of wrapping the sheets around a stuffing. First, I mixed the cheese, but it was too strong, so I added the ham, but it wasn't colorful, so I added the chives." The resulting pasta roll is quickly prepared, attractive, and flavorful.

In the same manner, Werner has introduced rabbit to his customers. He is gratified that it sells steadily. "I like it because it's close to what I remember as a kid. It's like my mother's."

In addition to handling special functions and room service in the hotel, Werner and his small staff cook for the Clift's French Room, a restaurant seating 110 people. The

Clift Hotel was first constructed in 1916, and its French Room has, since the beginning, signified a tradition of ornate dining. Despite remodeling, much remains of the original design, so the room still exudes an atmosphere of opulent luxury.

Soft sunlight filters through tall windows outlined by burgundy drapes. Three French-cut chandeliers dominate the ceiling. Coy nymphs and naughty cupids peek from above arching doorways. Deep carpets and plush chairs insulate against the din of downtown San Francisco. The French Room is the seventeenth-century—exclusive, refined, conscious of its antiquity and proud of its heritage.

To this symbol of virtuous tradition, Werner Albrecht has brought a young man's enthusiasm and a professional's knowledge. His command of classical cuisine and his exploration of contemporary ideas are ideally matched to ensure the Clift's continued reputation as one of San Francisco's best hotels. ✗

THE FRENCH ROOM
FOUR SEASONS CLIFT HOTEL, SAN FRANCISCO

MENU

CRAYFISH AND POACHED QUAIL EGGS SALAD WITH TRUFFLE VINAIGRETTE
Crayfish boiled in court bouillion, served with soft-boiled quail eggs, endive, and truffle dressing

CHEESE PASTA ROLL WITH TOMATO SAUCE
Spinach pasta stuffed and rolled with cream cheese, Ricotta, and Prosciutto, poached in chicken stock, and topped with fresh tomato sauce

RABBIT WITH APRICOTS IN CABERNET SAUCE
Boned rabbit stewed with apricots, garlic, and a Cabernet sauce

HIPPENNASSE
Baked egg, cream, and flour cup filled with fresh fruit of the season

✗

VINAIGRETTE
¼ ounce truffles
1 ounce red wine vinegar
3 ounces peanut oil
1 ounce shallots, finely chopped
1 bunch dill, chopped
salt and pepper to taste

In bowl, put truffles, shallots, dill, salt, and pepper. While whisking, add vinegar. Continue whisking and add oil to taste.

COURT BOUILLON
1 gallon water
8 ounces carrots
8 ounces celery
½ of single leek
2 cloves garlic
8 ounces onion
10 peppercorns
2 bay leaves
salt and pepper to taste

Coarsely chop all the vegetables. Place all ingredients in pot and cover with water. Cook over medium heat 20–25 minutes. Strain.

SALAD
1 gallon court bouillon
16 crayfish
8 quail eggs
1 head Belgian endive
1 head red chicory
vinaigrette dressing

In boiling water with a touch of vinegar, poach the quail eggs until soft. Place in a bowl with ice water to cool. Arrange endive and red chicory on plate. Decorate with quail eggs and crayfish tails. Serve with vinaigrette on the side.

TOMATO SAUCE
1 pound tomatoes
2 tablespoons butter
2 shallots, peeled and minced
bouquet garni—rosemary, thyme, bay
    leaf, crushed peppercorns
salt, freshly ground pepper

To prepare the tomatoes, drop them briefly into boiling water, then remove and plunge them into cold water and peel. Remove seeds and chop tomatoes. Melt butter in sauté pan and add minced shallots. Sauté, covered, for 5 minutes over low heat. Add tomatoes and bouquet garni. Season to taste. Cook covered over medium heat for 30 minutes. Remove shallots and bouquet garni, then purée. Reserve sauce.

PASTA ROLL

  2 tablespoons butter
½ cup smoked ham, diced
  4 scallions, minced
  8 ounces softened cream cheese
¼ cup Parmesan cheese
½ cup Ricotta cheese
½ teaspoon black pepper
  2 eggs
  2 sheets of fresh spinach pasta, 12 × 4 inches each
½ pound Prosciutto, ¼ inch thick
  1 gallon chicken stock
chives, chopped

In sauté pan, melt butter and add diced ham and scallions. Cook over medium heat about 2 minutes until scallions are soft. Beat cream cheese, Parmesan cheese, Ricotta cheese, and pepper together until smooth. Add sautéed ham and scallions to cheese mixture; then add eggs and mix well. Cover and refrigerate at least 2–3 hours. Spread half the filling on one pasta sheet leaving a half-inch border. Brush ends with melted butter. Place layer of sliced Prosciutto to cover mixture. Beginning at one of the short ends of the pasta, roll it up. Do not roll too loosely or the poaching liquid may seep into the cheese/meat mixture. Wrap roll in a double thickness of cheesecloth and tie each end securely with string. Repeat for second pasta sheet. Fill large sauté pan with chicken stock. Bring to a boil and add pasta rolls. Reduce heat to simmer and cook gently, turning ocassionally, for 25 minutes. Drain and cool before removing string and cheesecloth. Cut each roll in half-inch thick slices and arrange on plates. Pour tomato sauce on plate and add slices. Garnish with chopped chives. Serve warm or at room temperature.

Rabbit with Apricots in Cabernet Sauce

SERVINGS: 4
PREPARATION TIME: 1½ HOURS
MARINATE: 12 HOURS

1 young domestic rabbit
1 cup Cabernet Sauvignon
⅛ cup red wine vinegar
2 cloves garlic, unpeeled
bouquet garni
5 ounces dried apricots
coarse salt
freshly ground pepper
3 tablespoons peanut oil
4 tablespoons butter
1 cup rabbit demi-glace

Bone rabbit saddle, legs, and shoulders and cut the meat into cubes of about 1 ounce each. Marinate the meat in the wine and vinegar with garlic and bouquet garni for 12 hours, covering rabbit with cheesecloth so it will not dry out. Soak apricots in cold water for 1 hour, then drain. Drain rabbit, reserving marinade and garniture. Dry rabbit well and season with salt and pepper. In a heavy casserole, heat the oil and 2 tablespoons butter.

(continued)

Add the rabbit and brown on all sides (approximately 20 minutes until meat is gray). Add garlic, bouquet garni, reserved marinade, apricots, and rabbit demi-glace. Cut a circle of wax paper, butter it lightly, and place over the rabbit. Cover casserole and simmer 20–30 minutes. Remove bouquet garni and discard. Retrieve cloves of garlic and remove the peel. Mash garlic into a paste with the remaining butter. Remove rabbit and apricots from the sauce, set aside and keep warm. Stir the garlic paste into the sauce a little at a time. Arrange rabbit and apricots on serving plate and cover with sauce.

1⅛ cups whipping cream
13 ounces confectioners sugar
18 ounces flour
12 egg whites
fresh berries or fruit
strawberry or apricot purée
fresh mint leaves

In large bowl, combine egg whites and cream, then mix well with a whip. In a separate bowl, sieve together the confectioners sugar and flour. Slowly add the sugar-flour mixture to the egg whites and cream until a smooth paste is formed. Place a teaspoon at a time on a well-greased sheet pan. With the back of a spoon, spread the mixture to approximately 5 inches in diameter. Prepare the basket molds by greasing the bottoms of teacups. Bake cookies 2–3 minutes in a 375-degree oven. While still soft, mold into desired basket shapes, then continue baking until light brown and completely dry. Cool and store in air-tight container until used. To serve, fill cookie baskets with fresh fruit such as raspberries. Garnish with strawberry or apricot purée and fresh mint leaves.

CHEF MARK MILLER
FOURTH STREET GRILL

*D*uring the last decade, several restaurants in Berkeley, California have been major contributors to American culinary development. By taking advantage of the diverse cultural influences in the Bay Area and by utilizing an abundance of fresh and unusual food items, Berkeley chefs have devised a distinct cooking style owing its heritage to Oriental, European, and Latin American cultures.

Among the best of Berkeley restaurateurs is Mark Miller, who was an anthropology student when he began cooking at Alice Waters' Chez Panisse restaurant in Berkeley. In his three years as chef, he never repeated a menu. He also developed a solid basis for his own culinary philosophy.

As a result of his travels, particularly in the Yucatan region of Mexico, Mark formulated ideas for a restaurant that combined the tenets of simplicity and naturalness learned at Chez Panisse with the use of non-Western foods and cooking techniques.

For years, many San Francisco establishments have used mesquite for steaks and chops because its extremely high heat sears rapidly and seals in juices, imparting a subtle odor that does not distract from the food's normal flavors. As diners have become more knowledgeable, they have begun to demand cuisine that regains or enhances natural flavor, so mesquite cooking is now widely used in the Bay Area. It is a natural fuel, without chemicals, that can be used at very high temperatures to prepare fish or, with less heat, to cook meats.

Mark also notes that many of his customers are well-traveled and are willing to experiment with unusual foods. Thus his diners find chilis and peppers in abundance, scant salt, few dairy products, and an emphasis upon the simple, hearty, nourishing foods Mark loves.

Because he does not enjoy elaborately arrange foods and because his is country-style cooking, Mark does not concentrate on presentation. Still, basic colors are important, as are distinctions among flavors. "I like primary colors that give immediate response. And I like simple, assertive flavors. I have a classical cooking background that I try to integrate with non-Western ideas. Part of being a chef is to interpret or translate ideas."

This integration requires a willingness to utilize whatever is best and most appropriate. The essence of his approach to the business of eating is exemplified by his choice of beer, not wine, to accompany one of the dishes prepared for this program. "There are simply too many flavors in the appetizers to match with a wine. With all those chilis, the beer is refreshing and it's authentically regional."

There are no preconceptions and no slavish adherence to outdated rules at the Fourth Street Grill. Mark Miller has a direct, informed sense of what is needed to emphasize the best of each food.

The Fourth Street Grill is Mark's response to what he considers the obsolete practices of classical cuisine. "Nobody else in the world eats like Europeans. The Europeans eat too much of everything. In California, we have become eclectic. There is an emphasis here upon the integrity of natural flavors."

The restaurant itself is a physical manifestation of Mark's ideas. As if to repudiate sophisticated European design, it is squat and set amid railroad tracks and industrial buildings. Planter boxes with hybiscus and camellias add a needed touch of color. Inside, the decor is stark, with white walls, pale woods, dark carpet, and exposed wiring conduit.

In the kitchen, boxes are stacked in corners and extra chairs dangle from the ceiling. The centerpiece and heart of Mark's entire operation is a large, adjustable grill fired by mesquite charcoal. ✗

FOURTH STREET GRILL
BERKELEY

CHEF MARK MILLER
FOURTH STREET GRILL

MENU

SCALLOPS CEVICHE
Fresh scallops marinated in lime juice and served with garlic, peppers, chilies, and coriander

PEPPER OYSTERS
Fresh oysters poached in their own juice and served with a broth of garlic and black peppercorns

SWORDFISH ESCABECHE
Pickled swordfish sautéed in oil and served with a toasted garlic paste and vinegar sauce

OYSTERS WITH LIME-CHILI SAUCE
Oysters in their own shells with pepper and shallot relish

SALAD
Hearts of romaine, tomatillos, and avocado mixed with oil and lime juice

YUCATAN SEAFOOD STEW
Mussels, clams, angler fish, cod, tuna, squid, lobster, and oysters in a vegetable-fish broth

MANGO SORBET
Fresh mangos puréed and frozen

Scallops Ceviche

SERVINGS: 4
PREPARATION TIME: 1¼ HOURS

¾–1 pound fresh scallops
1 cup lime juice, to cover
2 cloves garlic, very finely chopped
1 sweet red bell pepper, deveined,
  seeded and julienned
2 sweet green chilies, deveined, seeded
  and julienned (may use an Anaheim
  chili as a substitute)
½ bunch coriander, stemmed and
  coarsely chopped
1 large tomato, cored and chopped
2 Jalapeño chilies (with seeds), finely
  chopped
½ cup olive oil

Slice scallops in thirds, cutting to
preserve shape and make a uniform
size. Place scallops into bowl, add
lime juice and marinate 1 hour.
After an hour, add garlic, red bell
pepper and sweet green chili. Mix
thoroughly. Add coriander, tomato,
and Jalapeño chilies. Add olive oil,
mix well, and serve immediately.
Do not keep more than 2–3 hours.

20–24 *fresh oysters*
2 *tablespoons black peppercorns*
3 *large garlic cloves, peeled*
½ *teaspoon salt*
3 *tablespoons olive oil*
3 *bay leaves*
2 *tablespoons fresh lime juice*

Shuck oysters and reserve shells and juice. Put oyster juice into a hot sauté pan and bring to a boil. Add oysters and poach gently 2–3 minutes until their edges curl slightly. Put peppercorns, garlic, and salt in a mortar and grind to a rough paste. Add ½ cup hot oyster juice to the mortar and continue to grind. Remove oysters from sauté pan and reserve. Add olive oil and bay leaves to liquid in pan and bring to a boil. Blend in mixture from mortar, then return oysters to pan and heat very briefly. Remove from heat and add lime juice. Turn onto serving plates and pour sauce over oysters. Serve cold or at room temperature. Refrigerate overnight for best flavor.

SERVINGS: 2
PREPARATION TIME: 45 MINUTES   MARINATE: 1 HOUR

2 fresh swordfish steaks, 8 ounces
   each
¼ cup fresh lime juice
1¼ cups water
1 teaspoon salt
¾ teaspoon oregano, toasted (Toast
   just until odor is noticeable, do not
   burn. Oregano will begin to smoke
   lightly when ready.)
2 bay leaves
2 whole allspice
⅓ teaspoon black peppercorns
½ teaspoon cumin seeds
1 clove
1 cinnamon stick
1 fresh garlic clove, peeled
½ teaspoon sugar
¾ cup red wine vinegar
¼ cup olive oil
½ sweet onion, sliced into thin rings
1–2 red chilies, sliced into thin rings

Marinate steaks in lime juice, water, and salt for 1 hour. In a grinder or mortar put toasted oregano, bay leaves, allspice, peppercorns, cumin seeds, whole clove, salt, coriander, cinnamon stick, fresh garlic clove, and sugar. Grind thoroughly, then add toasted garlic. Put mixture in sauté pan and add ¾ cup water, ½ cup red wine vinegar, and simmer for 15 minutes. Meanwhile, remove steaks from marinade, take off skins, cube, then pat dry. Heat another sauté pan, then add olive oil. Put swordfish into pan and sauté until it has a light, golden crust. Reserve swordfish on serving dish. Pour oil from pan and deglaze with ¼ cup red wine vinegar. Add herb and vinegar sauce to deglazed pan and bring to a boil. Add a touch of water if sauce becomes too thick. Spoon sauce over fish and garnish with sweet onions and red chilies. Serve at room temperature.

SERVINGS: 4
PREPARATION TIME: 15 MINUTES

1 dozen oysters, shucked and shells
   reserved
1–2 large fresh shallots
½ bunch fresh coriander
1 fresh Jalapeño chili, deveined and
   seeded
1 red chili, deveined and seeded
⅓–½ cup fresh lime juice

Place raw oysters on their half shells on serving plate. Dice the remaining ingredients to approximately the same size (not too fine). Place in a bowl with the lime juice and mix. Dab relish on tops of oysters and serve.

hearts of 2 heads of Romaine lettuce
4 tomatilloes, sliced (or use fresh green
     tomatoes)
2 medium tomatoes, sliced
2 Haas avocados, sliced
2 tablespoons fresh lime juice
½ cup olive oil
1 bunch coriander

Place lettuce, tomatilloes, tomatoes, and avocado in large bowl. Sprinkle with lime juice and olive oil, but do not toss. Garnish with coriander leaves to taste.

SERVINGS: 6–8
PREPARATION TIME: 1½ HOURS

¾ cup olive oil
1 medium onion, chopped
1 large head garlic, roasted and
   chopped
3 bay leaves
2 allspice, crushed
1½–2 quarts fish stock (or chicken
   stock)
3 bunches coriander
8 clams, Manilla or Littleneck
8 large tomatoes, grilled until almost
   black, roughly chopped
8 ounces angler fish (monk fish)
½ cup fresh lime juice
2 Pasilla chilies, roasted, peeled, skin
   stripped off, and julienned (2
   Chipotle or Jalapeño chilies can be
   substituted)
1 dozen mussels, scrubbed and
   debearded
8 ounces tuna filet
8 ounces rock cod filet
8 ounces ling cod filet
1 lobster, 1½–2 pounds, parboiled
8 shrimp, parboiled
4 large oysters, removed from shell
4 small fresh squid

Heat large sauté pan and add olive oil. Sauté onion, toasted garlic, cloves, bay leaves, and allspice for about 10 minutes. (Do not brown.) Meanwhile, heat fish stock in a saucepan.

To the sauté pan, add 1 bunch coriander (tied together), all of the clams, and the grilled tomatoes. Turn heat to high and bring to a boil. Then add 2 cups heated fish stock, cover, and steam to open clams (about 5 minutes). Replenish fish stock as needed to keep ingredients covered. Add angler fish, lime juice (to taste), and chilies. If necessary, add more coriander and roasted garlic. Continue cooking for 2 minutes, then bring to a rolling boil and add mussels. (Note: Mussels open quickly.) Add remainder of fish (tuna and cod), then lobster, shrimp, oysters, and squid. (Note: All fish should have the skin removed and be cut into 1-inch cubes.) Remove tied bunch of coriander, then cook covered for 2–3 minutes and serve. Garnish with fresh coriander.

SERVINGS: 4–6
PREPARATION TIME: 30 MINUTES   CHILL: UNTIL FREEZING

2 cups mango, puréed
2 tablespoons simple syrup (1 cup water
   and 1 cup sugar)
2 tablespoons fresh lime juice

Strain puréed mangos through a chinois (sieve) and add simple syrup, then lime juice. Using an ice-cream maker, chill and churn until frozen.

CHEF ROBERTO GEROMETTA
CHEZ MICHEL

*I*n his European training and his broad work experience, Roberto Gerometta is representative of San Francisco's cosmopolitan cooking tradition and of the diversity found in the city's finest restaurant kitchens. Born near Venice, Italy, educated in France where he attended design and culinary schools, Roberto has worked in Europe, in the Bahamas, in New York City at La Caravelle, in Los Angeles at L'Hérmitage, and in Seattle where he had his own restaurant. He is now in San Francisco, at

Chez Michel, a beautiful showcase set beside cable car tracks leading down to San Francisco Bay.

The restaurant is a pleasing blend of decorative fabrics, pale woods, and brass. Its two dining rooms, full bar, and airy spaciousness are redolent of contemporary French design elegance. Particularly striking are vivid, multi-colored fabric ceiling panels. Like a summer pavillion cooled by gentle breezes, the dining rooms beneath the fabrics are gracious and comfortable, enfolding the diner in a welcoming cocoon of contentment.

The restaurant's design is ideally suited to Roberto's talents. Because the cooking area is open to one of the dining rooms, the chef is always on view. And because Roberto is a lively, personable man who works well under pressure, he thrives in the stage atmosphere of that kitchen.

The menu is principally Roberto's creation but is more a reflection of what the clientele want than what he would like to offer. Filet mignon, onion soup, rack of lamb, and steak tartare are expected. Roberto favors more variety but believes his customers are not yet ready for great inventiveness. Consequently, he seeks to marry traditional fare with new, subtle tastes.

For this television series, he decided upon a mousseline of frog legs and stuffed leg of duck. Then, as if to test the supremecy of his training, and in defiance of his own assertion that he really did not care for desserts, he executed the Progrès au Grand Marnier, an elaborate, difficult chocolate confection. The success of the meal is an indication of Roberto's professional, polished approach to cooking.

Roberto comments frequently upon the quality of ingredients in California. He mentions specifically the white asparagus, formerly available only as a French import, and the fresh produce. But unlike many of his contemporaries, he is suspicious of herbs, which are gaining increasing popularity in many kitchens. "I'm not crazy about spices. They have to be used the right way. Sometimes people overuse spices, to hide something. You know, spices are our enemy sometimes."

He also appreciates other advantages to living in California. With his wife, he owns a house in a small town near San Francisco where he spends much of his time in the yard. "Gardening is my passion. I raise herbs, flowers, even olive trees."

As he talks, Roberto gestures emphatically with his hands and emphasizes his thoughts with little puffs of air blown between pursed lips. Cooking has provided him a pleasurable life, but he has worked very hard for his achievements. He spent long hours as a young apprentice learning the intricacies of his profession, and he has little patience with the legions of amateurs who would open their own restaurants without sufficient training. "Sure, the dream of any chef is to own his own restaurant, but so many don't understand the pressure. You have to give up a lot, and you need dedication."

Still, he finds great joy in the process of refining his skills. "Anybody can cook. The important difference is to keep learning." He will spend hours perfecting a new menu item to please his customers. "I think that's the surprise of a new dish. Something about which people will say 'Wow, this is great.' That makes *me* feel great." ✗

CHEZ MICHEL
SAN FRANCISCO

MENU

MOUSSELINE OF FROG LEGS WITH FRESH PASTA
Small mousse of frog legs served over fresh pasta with special frog-leg sauce

STUFFED LEG OF DUCK WITH RED WINE SAUCE
Leg of duck stuffed with chicken livers, bacon, pork, and truffles, baked, then served with Volnay and duck sauce

PROGRÈS WITH GRAND MARNIER
Elegant layers of meringue, buttercream, hazelnut cream, and chocolate mousse

✗

Mousseline of Frog Legs with Fresh Pasta

SERVINGS: 4
PREPARATION TIME: 2 HOURS

7 tablespoons butter
2 shallots, chopped
3 pounds frog legs
½ bottle dry white wine
salt and pepper
1 pint heavy cream (may need a little
   more)
4 ounces filet of sole
1 egg
½ lemon
1 tablespoon olive oil
½ pound fresh pasta
1 bunch chives

In sauté pan heat 2 tablespoons butter. Sauté shallots in butter until they are golden brown. Add 1½ pounds frog legs, white wine, salt and pepper. Cover and cook slowly for 10 minutes. Strain, debone, and reserve legs. Replace strained stock in sauté pan, add ¼ quart cream and reduce by half.

Debone remaining frog legs. Place in meat grinder or food processor with sole and grind thoroughly. Add egg, salt and pepper, and 1 cup cream (adjust to taste). Process mousseline and reserve.

Take reserved frog leg sauce, bring to boil, and add heavy cream

(continued)

to adjust consistency. If sauce is too thick, thin with white wine. Add butter, lemon juice, salt and pepper.

Boil salted water, add olive oil and pasta. When pasta is *al dente*, strain and cool under running water. Reserve.

Butter four molds. Put mousseline into pastry bag and squeeze into molds, leaving hole in center. Fill center with frog leg meat and top with mousseline. Tamp gently to remove trapped air bubbles. Place in pan with layer of water about 1 inch deep. On top of mold, place layer of buttered parchment, then a layer of foil. Cook in oven for 15 minutes at 400 degrees.

To serve, sauté pasta in 3 table-spoons butter, adjust seasoning, then layer on serving plates. Re-move mousseline from molds and place on pasta. Pour sauce over mousseline and sprinkle with chopped chives.

STUFFED LEG OF DUCK WITH RED WINE SAUCE

SERVINGS: 2
PREPARATION TIME: 2 HOURS

SAUCE AND ASSEMBLY
1 *whole duck (4½–5 pounds) or 2 duck legs*
6 *tablespoons olive oil*
1 *onion*
1 *carrot*
1 *tomato*
1 *pinch thyme*
1 *bay leaf*
6 *black peppercorns*
½ *bottle red wine (Volnay)*
8 *ounces veal or duck stock*
1 *pound white turnips*
2 *ounces butter*
3 *ounces caul fat*

Debone duck, reserve legs for this dish and remainder of duck for an-other dish. Chop bones and place in heavy pan with heated olive oil. Add onion and carrot, then brown. Add quartered tomato, thyme, bay leaf, peppercorns, and salt. Deglaze with red wine and veal stock, then cook approximately 1 hour. Strain sauce and reserve.

Peel turnips and shape into small spears. Place in small saucepan, cover with water, add butter and salt, then bring to a boil. When liq-uid is almost evaporated, add ½ teaspoon sugar. Continue to cook until a brown glaze forms in pan.

(continued)

Deglaze pan with ¼ cup duck sauce and reserve for garnish.

Debone duck leg and pound meat flat. Lay caul fat on flat surface and cut into 5 by 5 inch squares. Place deboned leg on each square, salt and pepper the meat. Place stuffing (recipe follows) in center of each leg. Close leg over stuffing and caul fat over leg, shaping in the form of a chop. Place in a buttered pan and cook in 450- to 500-degree oven for 20 to 25 minutes. Heat reserved sauce, whipping in small pieces of cold butter. Adjust seasoning.

To serve, slice duck and place in center of plate, garnish with turnips and add sauce.

STUFFING

2 ounces pork
2 ounces bacon
1 ounce chicken liver
1 shallot, chopped
1 ounce butter
1 egg yolk
1 truffle
2 tablespoons heavy cream—varies
  according to amount of fat in pork
salt and pepper

Put pork, bacon, and chicken liver through meat grinder. In sauté pan, heat butter and cook shallot. In bowl, mix chopped meats, shallot, egg yolk, chopped truffle, cream, salt and pepper.

BISCUIT NOISETTE

6 egg whites
small pinch of salt
1 ounce lemon juice
1 ounce sugar
½–1 ounce flour
5 ounces hazlenuts, finely ground
5 ounces sugar

Put egg whites into blender with salt and lemon juice. Add 1 ounce sugar to egg whites while blending. In separate bowl, blend flour, 5 ounces sugar and ground hazlenuts. Add beaten egg whites to bowl with hazlenut/sugar mixture and fold in with spatula. Butter bottom of baking sheet, cover with buttered parchment paper. Pour biscuit dough on parchment and place in 500-degree oven for 5 minutes, turning often. When cooked, cool in refrigerator.

SYRUP

4 ounces water
4 ounces sugar
1 ounce Grand Marnier

In small saucepan, bring water and sugar to boil. Take off heat and cool in refrigerator. Add Grand Marnier to cooled syrup and re-serve. (Note: Three-fourths of this syrup–Grand Marnier mixture will be used in the mousse; the remainder will be used to bunch the various layers of the Progrès.

BUTTERCREAM

1 pint milk
10 egg yolks
10 ounces sugar
26 ounces butter

Heat milk in saucepan. In bowl, whisk together egg yolks and sugar. Add heated milk to egg/sugar mix-ture and whisk off heat. Put mix-ture back in saucepan and whisk while heating, until smooth and fairly thick. Remove from heat and strain back into bowl. Cool in refrig-erator. When chilled, remove from refrigerator and place in blender. While blending on low speed, add butter a little at a time. Blend until smooth, then return to refrigerator.

CREME NOISETTE

¼ of the buttercream (see above)
1 ounce hazlenut paste (or almond paste)
1 teaspoon Kirsch

MOUSSE

1 pint heavy cream
4 egg yolks
½–¾ cup syrup–Grand Marnier (see above)
4 ounces chocolate, melted

CHOCOLATE CREAM

remaining buttercream (see above)
12 ounces chocolate

ASSEMBLY

Put hazlenut paste and Kirsch into bowl and mix with a spatula. Add 4 ounces of buttercream and blend well. Refrigerate for 5 minutes.

Whip cream with whisk. In another bowl, over hot water, whisk egg yolks and syrup. Add melted chocolate to whipped cream and whisk until smooth. Fold egg/syrup mixture into chocolate/cream mixture and mix with spatula.

Melt chocolate, then cool. Add half of the chocolate to the buttercream. Mix well, then add remainder of chocolate (must be done in steps or cream will break). Refrigerate.

Remove biscuit from refrigerator and cut to shape of mold. Put bottom biscuit into mold and brush with syrup. Spread layer of creme noisette on top of syrup. Refrigerate for 2 minutes. Add a layer of mousse, then place top biscuit on mousse. Brush with syrup again, then spread with a layer of chocolate cream. Freeze for 5–30 minutes. Pipe layer of chocolate cream on top. Unmold and serve on tray with garnish of sugar and real flowers.

95

CHEF ADRIANA GIRAMONTI
GIRAMONTI RESTAURANT

*D*uring World War II, Adriana Giramonti was stranded in a small Italian village near Monte Casino. Her memories of that time are with her still. The fear, the noise of combat, and, above all, the hunger, form a somber backdrop to her daily life and give impetus to her cooking. Unwillingly, she recalls the day when the German troops began their retreat, stripping the village of food and material. "There was no food because we couldn't cultivate the fields. We were always hungry. That's one of the reasons I enjoy food now. I remember those days."

With her mother in Rome, Adriana learned how to feed large groups of people simply and well. One of five children, the young girl early acquired a familiarity with the Roman markets and with recipes that were quick, yet wonderfully flavorful.

At the age of twenty-seven, she came to California, where she found work in a San Francisco Italian restaurant. In twenty years as a waitress, she picked up the essentials of restaurant cooking and operations, and she also married Nino, who has been a waiter in several San Francisco restaurants. Together they opened Giramonti Restaurant in 1977.

An excellent cook himself, Nino supervises Giramonti's two small dining rooms. He is a wine enthusiast particularly interested in matching his wife's cooking style with Italian and California wines. The husband and wife have found an excellent balance in running what is essentially a very busy family restaurant, or *trattoria.*

It is an apt description. One wall is glass, giving a relaxing view of an inlet of San Francisco Bay backed by the green beauty of Mt. Tamalpais. The decor is eclectic, with an air of family enterprise in the still-life paintings by Adriana, the display of small decorative plates and molds, the patterned blue wallpaper, and the informal hospitality.

Since Italy is the wellspring of Adriana's creativity, Giramonti's menus bear the initials S.P.Q.R., the inscription seen throughout Rome on public works and municipal buildings. The letters represent a Latin motto translated roughly as "For the People of Rome," a phrase perfectly descriptive of Adriana's Roman culinary heritage and her cooking method, which is essentially home-style permeated by love and intelligent care.

"When we first opened, I was going to do just a few things very well, but the more I cooked, the more I remembered what my mother had taught me about putting together the right things, herbs and other ingredients, with lots of love."

Four items are essential to Adriana's cooking: chicken broth, occasionally mixed with beef stock; tomato sauce; a Roman-style brown gravy; and white wine. She also favors basil, parsley, sage, rosemary, and marjoram. Each day she makes fresh stocks to use in recipes for several pastas accompanied by a variety of meat and fish; for minestrone soup containing no tomatoes but generous amounts of fresh vegetables; for sautéd chicken; and, of course, for veal in several styles.

Adriana smiles self-indulgently when describing her fondness for veal. "I must say that I am very good with veal. I have invented many dishes with it." Her Veal Adriana is an excellent case in point, its piquant mustard and cream sauce a precise counterpoint to the veal's delicate flavor.

To create a new recipe, Adriana need only recall her childhood years in Italy. "I remember what I ate as a child in Rome. I picture myself in my grandparents' house with clouds of smoke in the kitchen and everyone cooking."

She is refreshingly enthusiastic about food and admits that her desire to cook has actually increased recently, as though the passage of years has heightened her appreciation for the fundamental goodness and pleasures of food. "Every day now I can create something new. I love to handle the food. I am more and more excited about food all the time." ✗

GIRAMONTI RESTAURANT
MILL VALLEY, MARIN COUNTY

MENU

ARTICHOKES ROMAN STYLE
Artichokes and sweet onions with lemon and marjoram

EMPRESS MUSHROOMS
Sautéed mushrooms with Prosciutto and herbs

MARINATED EGGPLANT
Sliced eggplant, simmered in red vinegar, then layered in soufflé dish

CROSTINI WITH CHICKEN LIVERS
Chicken livers sautéed in white wine and cream, then served on small French bread toasts

LINGUINE "DELIZIOSE"
Linguine with sautéed prawns, salmon, leeks, and mushrooms

VEAL ADRIANA
Thin slices of veal simmered in mustard, cream, and white wine

STRAWBERRIES ITALIAN STYLE
Strawberries marinated in white wine and Port

✗

Artichokes Roman Style

SERVINGS: 4
PREPARATION TIME: 45 MINUTES

12 *small artichokes*
 1 *lemon*
 2 *medium onions, quartered*
 1 *clove garlic, chopped*
 1 *teaspoon dried marjoram*
¼ *cup olive oil*
 1 *cup chicken broth*
salt and pepper

Remove outer leaves of artichokes, cut off tops, and let artichokes stand in cold water with juice of the lemon for 10 minutes. Arrange artichokes around sides of heavy casserole. Put quartered onions in middle. Sprinkle with garlic, marjoram, oil, broth, salt and pepper. Cover and bring to boil over high heat. Simmer gently over low heat, still covered, for 20 minutes. Serve.

EMPRESS MUSHROOMS

SERVINGS : 4
PREPARATION TIME: 30 MINUTES

16 medium mushrooms
1 small onion, chopped
1 garlic clove, chopped
½ cup olive oil
6 ounces Prosciutto or 1 large slice
   ham
2 teaspoons parsley
2 teaspoons marjoram
salt and pepper
1 cup white wine
bread crumbs
grated Parmigiano cheese

Clean mushrooms thoroughly; remove amd chop stems. Sauté onions and garlic in ¼ cup olive oil until transparent. Add chopped mushrooms stems, chopped prosciutto, parsley, marjoram, salt and pepper. Sauté for about 1½ minutes, then add wine. Add bread crumbs until mixture is consistency of mush. Coat mushroom tops with remaining olive oil. Stuff each mushroom with tablespoon of mixture, then sprinkle with Parmigiano cheese and bake at 375 degrees for 3–7 minutes, depending upon size of the mushrooms.

MARINATED EGGPLANT

SERVINGS: 4–6
PREPARATION TIME: 30 MINUTES

1 eggplant
4 eggs
1–2 teaspoons parsley, chopped
6 bay leaves
1 teaspoon rosemary, optional
3 garlic cloves, crushed
2½ cups olive oil
½ cup red wine vinegar
flour, salt, pepper

Cut eggplant in slices about ¾ inch thick. Arrange on dishtowel side by side, sprinkle with salt, let rest 10 minutes, and wipe dry. Reserve.

In bowl, beat eggs with parsley, pinch of salt, and pepper. Heat 2 cups oil. Flour eggplant slices lightly, then dip in egg wash. Sauté in hot oil until golden brown, about 1 minute each side. Place on absorbent towel to cool.

Meanwhile, in heavy saucepan, place remaining oil with crushed garlic. Sauté until garlic is golden. Remove from heat and add vinegar. Return to heat and add bay leaves, rosemary, and pepper to taste, then simmer 1 minute. Reserve.

In bowl with lid, assemble one layer of eggplant then sprinkle with marinated sauce. Add another layer

of eggplant and sprinkle with marinade. Continue process until all eggplant is used then pour remaining marinade over whole dish. Cover, then turn upside down to mix marinade. Marinate for at least 2 hours at room temperature. Unmold on serving plate and serve at room temperature. Will keep in refrigerator for two weeks.

SERVINGS: 6
PREPARATION TIME: 30 MINUTES

2 tablespoons butter
olive oil
1 small onion, chopped
1 garlic clove, chopped
½ pound chicken livers, chopped very
  fine
½ cup white wine
salt and pepper
1½–2 teaspoons parsley
⅕ cup heavy cream
½ cup brown gravy (veal stock and
  herbs)
1 small loaf french bread, cut in ¼-
  inch slices

In a sauté pan, put 1 tablespoon butter, some olive oil, the onion and garlic. Sauté lightly until onion is transparent. Add chopped livers and sauté well over high heat for about 3 minutes or less. Add white wine, salt, pepper, and parsley. As soon as wine has evaporated, add cream, 1 tablespoon butter, and the brown gravy, then simmer on low heat for about 1 minute.

Slice French bread very thin (use day-old bread) then roast it on a baking pan in oven for 1 minute. Spread liver mixture on bread to serve. Garnish with grated white truffle, sautéed mushrooms, or chopped parsley.

LINGUINE "DELIZIOSE"

1 pound linguine
1 pound medium prawns, cleaned and
    deveined
1 pound fresh salmon fillet, julienned
    coarsely
flour
½–¾ cup olive oil
1 cup leeks, julienned
6 ounces mushrooms, sliced
½ cup white wine
1 tablespoon marjoram
1 tablespoon parsley, chopped
2 garlic cloves, crushed and chopped
salt and pepper
2 tablespoons butter, optional
1 cup chicken broth

Boil linguine according to package instructions or make fresh. Cool under cold running water and reserve.

Flour prawns and salmon lightly. In large sauté pan, heat oil over high heat, then add prawns and salmon and sauté for 1 minute. Add leeks and mushrooms (one at a time), sauté for 1 minute after each addition. Next, add wine, marjoram, parsley, garlic, salt, pepper, and butter. Sauté lightly. Add broth, lower heat and simmer for 2 minutes, adding more broth if it becomes too dry. Add drained linguine and mix well, then simmer for 1 minute.

To serve, place linguine on plate first, decorate with prawns, then pour remaining sauce over both. Garnish with parsley.

VEAL ADRIANA

MUSTARD SAUCE
2–3 tablespoons Dijon mustard
juice of 1 lemon
6 ounces heavy cream
salt and white pepper to taste

Mix all ingredients in bowl to form smooth sauce.

VEAL
1 pound veal scaloppine, pounded thin
flour
olive oil
1 cup white wine
¼ cup chicken broth
¼ cup brown gravy
mustard sauce
chopped parsley

Lightly flour veal slices. In sauté pan, warm oil, then sauté veal for 1 minute on each side. Drain oil and add wine to pan (do not cover veal with wine). Bring liquid to boil, then lower heat and add chicken broth, brown gravy, and mustard sauce. Add 1 teaspoon chopped parsley and simmer for 3–4 minutes. Remove veal slices to serving dish. If sauce is too thick, add broth; if too thin, add some cream. Heat sauce well and pour over veal. Garnish with chopped parsley.

SERVINGS: 10–12
PREPARATION TIME: 1½ HOURS

3 baskets of strawberries or peaches (or combination of both)
1 cup sugar
2 fresh lemons
1 orange
½ cup Port and/or sweet vermouth
1 cup white wine

Wash strawberries, remove tops, and peel peaches. Slice in medium-sized pieces. Add to bowl and sprinkle sugar over fruit. Add lemon juice, orange juice, Port, and wine. Mix and refrigerate at least 1 hour. Serve in chilled glass cups.

Left to right: Booby Floyd, trombone; Freddie Kohlman, drums; Danny Rubio, tuba; Phamous Lambert, piano; Mike Sizer, clarinet; and Frank Trapani, trumpet. (Not pictured: Julie Rubio, vocalist.)

Food and music are synonymous with New Orleans, where the Great Chefs series originated, so naturally each of the Great Chefs shows opens and closes with Dixieland jazz. The world-famous Dukes of Dixieland have been a New Orleans establishment since 1949. Their versatility and innate musicianship is such that they have included non-Dixieland music as well throughout the Great Chefs series.

The Dukes remain today one of the best proponents of New Orleans jazz. They perform nightly in their French Quarter nightclub, "Dukes' Place." In the course of a year they present sixty concerts, appearing with major symphonies and festivals in the great concert halls of the world.

In the past two decades, guitarist Charlie Byrd has emerged as a giant on the international music scene. Working with equal ease in both classical music and jazz, Byrd and his trio added their special flavor to the Great Chefs of San Francisco television series. The technical proficiency derived from his classical training has opened up a new level of performance for Charlie Byrd—jazz played on a classical guitar without a pick or amplification.

Following a distinguished career studded with many honors, in 1980 Byrd and a group of his friends opened "Charlie's," a beautiful jazz and supper club in Georgetown, D.C. He continues to spend a portion of each year on the road, bring out new recordings, and write scores for films, television, modern dance and theatre.

ACKNOWLEDGEMENTS

✗

	PUBLISHER	AVON BOOKS THE HEARST CORPORATION
	PROPRIETORS	WYES-TV, NEW ORLEANS TELE-RECORD PRODUCTIONS, LTD.

BOOK PRODUCTION

EDITORIAL AND PRODUCTION SERVICES	JACK JENNINGS AND JUDY JOHNSTONE BMR, SAN FRANCISCO
WRITER	CHARLES ROBBINS
RESEARCHER	TERRI HINRICHS
CONSULTING CHEF	DANIEL BONNOT
CHEF COORDINATOR	JOHN LODER
DESIGN	MICHAEL PATRICK CRONAN
CALLIGRAPHY	GEORGIA DEAVER
PHOTOGRAPHY	ROBIN RYAN
PUBLIC RELATIONS	LINDA NIX LESLIE RUBIN SALLY SHEPARD CANDICE JACOBSON

TELEVISION PRODUCTION

TELEVISION PRODUCER AND WRITER	JOHN BEYER
ASSOCIATE PRODUCER	TERRI HINRICHS
DIRECTOR	DAVE LANDRY
NARRATORS	MARY LOU CONROY ANDRES CALANDRIA
VIDEO EFFECTS	JIM MORIARTY
VIDEOTAPE EDITOR	JULIUS EVANS
ENGINEERING	C. CALDWELL SAINZ STEVE HOWELL
CAMERA	JIM LYNCH
AUDIO	PETER J. LUDÉ
FIELD ENGINEER	RUDY MONTANO
EXECUTIVE PRODUCER	JOHN SHOUP
MUSIC	CHARLIE BYRD TRIO THE DUKES OF DIXIELAND JULIE RUBIO, VOCALIST
HEADQUARTER HOTEL FOR GREAT CHEFS PRODUCTION TEAM	THE FOUR SEASONS CLIFT